On Writing,
Editing, and Publishing

Chicago Guides
to *Writing*, Editing
and Publishing

Already Published

Writing for Social Scientists
How to Start and Finish Your Thesis, Book, or Article
Howard S. Becker, with a chapter by Pamela Richards

The Craft of Translation
Edited by John Biguenet and Rainer Schulte

Chicago Guide to Preparing Electronic Manuscripts
For Authors and Publishers
Prepared by the Staff of the University of Chicago Press

Getting into Print
The Decision-Making Process
Walter W. Powell

A Manual for Writers of Term Papers, Theses,
and Dissertations
Fifth Edition
Kate Turabian, revised and enlarged by
Bonnie Birtwistle Honigsblum

Tales of the Field
On Writing Ethnography
John Van Maanen

A Handbook of Biological Illustration
Second Edition
Frances W. Zweifel

Jacques Barzun
On Writing,
Editing, and Publishing

Essays Explicative and Hortatory
Second Edition

With a Foreword by Morris Philipson

The University of Chicago Press

Chicago and London

The University of Chicago Press, Chicago 60637
The University of Chicago Press, Ltd., London

© 1971, 1986 by The University of Chicago
All rights reserved
Published 1971
Second edition, expanded 1986
Printed in the United States of America

95 94 93 92 91 90   5

Library of Congress Cataloging-in-Publication Data

Barzun, Jacques, 1907–
    On writing, editing, and publishing.

    1. Authorship—Addresses, essays, lectures.
    2. Authors and publishers—Addresses, essays, lectures.
    I. Title.
PN149.B295   1986   808'.02   85–16562
ISBN 0–226–03857–2 (cloth)
ISBN 0–226–03858–0 (paper)

Contents

Foreword

Of making many books there may be no end, but of making them any better there is almost no means. Publishing, editing, and writing remain cottage industries in which apprenticeship offers the only approximation to specialized training. Publishing, being a business, offers the most objective conditions for teaching and for evaluating how successfully the trainee is learning his job; editing, too, less sharply defined but seeking to be a profession, offers some opportunities for knowing whether one is learning one's trade; but writing, at least a craft and at its best an art, aspiring to the unique, is the most difficult of all to learn.

Nevertheless, standards do exist and guides are available. They may be partial and personal and as difficult to come by as the autobiographical essays of the Russian writer Zamyatin, in *A Soviet Heretic,* or as impersonal and encyclopedic and readily available as the Chicago *Manual of Style.* But the hints, the counsel, the advice are so profoundly needed that anyone who is interested in the written word—even those who already may know Fowler's *Dictionary of Modern English Usage,* Strunk and White's *Elements of Style,* Gowers's *Complete Plain Words,* Follett's *Modern American Usage*—may now rejoice in having available this collection of fugitive essays, these exposés, plaints, and onslaughts, from the pen of one of the wittiest of wise men, one of the best writers who ever set himself to (as it looks only at the outset) the unrewarding task of writing about writing.

In the autumn of 1970 I read a review by Jacques Barzun in the *American Scholar* which started me thinking again of the number of scattered articles of his, read over the past two dozen years, which sounded variations on the common theme of the glories and miseries of writing-editing-publishing. It struck me that it would be well worth while to bring the fugitive pieces together as a book. Though responsive to the suggestion, Mr. Barzun felt strongly that unless I would take the responsibility for editing these papers and seeing them through the press, he was not disposed to make a gathering of them. Respecting all three activities to which the essays are addressed, and in which I could become engaged simultaneously, I found the invitation irresistible.

True to the classic conditions of publishing, the author and the editor then fell into a disagreement. I wanted to call the book *Advice to Would-be Writers, Editors, and Publishers.* The author wrote back saying, "*Advice to* strikes me as wrong and misleading. Except for the one paragraph written ad hoc, there is no advice given in my pieces, but description, expostulation, and fantastication. Nor can I be represented as advising now with old pieces. Something like *Wisdom for* would seem more exact and, curiously enough, more modest." In effect, you see Barzun in operation. The overriding concern is for precision, rightness of tone, and effectiveness of communication. But of course in conflicts between publishers and authors, while the publisher's first concern may be for what is most attractive commercially, the author's first concern, frequently enough, is for accuracy—and sometimes for modesty.

Now consider the difference between advice and wisdom. To my mind, wisdom is what enables one to bear the inevitable; it offers the solace of recognizing and accepting the limits of doing. With wisdom one can endure what is necessary, inescapable, unchangeable. It is retrospective and essentially theoretical. Advice, on the other hand, is prospective and essentially practical. It offers counsel on altering for the better what is still subject to change. Deliberate counsel given through wise judgments, enabling one to alter future actions, makes advice useful.

If these essays by Jacques Barzun are not advice in the explicit sense—rules, programs, statements of standards —they most certainly are that by implication. They invariably teach us by examples which entertain as they instruct, for just as they deflate pretension and excoriate ignorance, so do they extol honesty and honor integrity.

(As to the conclusion of the conflict between author and publisher with regard to the title of this work, you have the answer in your hands.)

Are honesty and integrity then the concepts these essays are ultimately founded upon? I think so. Because, as I read them, they are stalwart by virtue of being grounded in the most significant purpose of language: communication between people—or, ideally, communion among people. Barzun's crucial terms of evaluation are moral, not aesthetic. What is execrable is what misleads, what traduces, what injects error, what cloaks the absence of thought or feeling, what pretends to be something other than it is, what is false.

Barzun's aesthetic concern is always to use language as a transparent medium. The ideal is for the medium to have no message at all. The only message of any importance whatsoever is the feeling or thought to be communicated. The metaphor in the phrase "clarity of expression" names the condition that enables one to "see through" flawlessly to what is meant.

Where transparency of the medium is coupled with density of thought or richness of feeling, Barzun argues, the contrast yields eloquence, the greatest power inherent in the artful use of language.

In personal relations the analogue of eloquence is the power to charm. Charming another (unlike merely entertaining him) enriches that person through such fascinating communication as enhances his sense of vital experience. He is made wiser or warmer for it—"more alive." The opposite of charm is not dullness, it is spite: for a spiteful remark diminishes the other person, and in wreaking spitefulness one deliberately goes out of the way to make someone else feel poorer or smaller or weaker—"less alive." We are offered precious little in our formal or informal education to help us cultivate the power to charm, and, similarly, there are all too few counsels to help writers cultivate the power of effectiveness, let alone eloquence. Both activities require one to "go out of the way" in order to achieve the desirable purposes, especially if the conventional "way" is cluttered with obstacles making for muddiness or cloudiness or phoniness—as, in personal relations, there might be obstructive attitudes of meanness or unkindness or other variations of viciousness.

By concentrating on the meanings which a writer wishes to communicate, Barzun instructs by remaining always true to the principle of "protecting the work and not the self." By setting his sights always on the ultimate purpose of enhancing the writer's power to see things

plain and to express them clearly, he offers the wisdom
of recognizing accurately the powers and limits of verbal
communication. In the compassion of his wisdom and
the eloquence of his exposition lie the seeds of advice for
every fertile mind.

MORRIS PHILIPSON, Director
The University of Chicago Press

Introductory:
Advice to a Young Writer

The first question for the young writer to ask himself is: "Have I things in my head which I need to set forth, or do I merely want to be a writer?" Another way of putting it is, "Do I want to write—or *to have written?*" The ambition to be known as a writer is not in itself unworthy, but it requires a deliberate search for likely subjects and a strong effort of thought and will to turn them into copy.

For a born writer the effort is altogether different. It is merely to choose from an abundance of ideas those which he thinks he is fit to handle—fit, that is, by reason of study, experience, and literary skill. This last element is getting scarcer, it would seem, so that readers have to get cleverer at guessing riddles. Hence practicing to write well and finally writing well will repay. Editors and publishers will seek you out, the public will be carried away with love and gratitude.

But these rewards presuppose that what is well written also concerns the lives and minds of your contemporaries. This relationship does not limit you to current events or fashionable ideas, to the newspaper headlines or the jargon of your profession. Rather, to be a writer and not a hack, you must clear your mind of cant and allow multitudinous messages to come to you from the souls of your fellowmen. They are the secret source of your abundant ideas. People do not know what they communicate; yet it is they whom you "read," con-

sciously and unconsciously, and whom you interpret to
themselves, in stories, poems, plays, or works of social
and moral philosophy.

[1969]

A Writer to His Mates

1   A Writer's Discipline

No writer has ever lived who did not at some time or other get stuck. Even the great producers such as Scott and Dickens suffered from the professional malady of being "for no good reason" (as we all say) unable to write. And for every writer in working trim there may be a dozen persons of great ability who are somehow self-silenced. At long intervals they turn out remarkable fragments—half-essays or embryo stories; but they cannot seem to pull themselves together and finish anything, much less begin at will.

Now writing is not an art in which one can succeed by the production of interesting ruins, and since the total or partial paralysis of the writer's will is a fearsome and mysterious blight, most writers come to recognize the need of a discipline, a set of ritual practices which will put the momentum of habit behind their refractory ego and push them over the obstacle. Scott confessed that he used his divided self in order to rule: hating the thought of commitment, he hardly ever wrote anything except to flee the necessity of writing something else. And Dickens tells of long mornings when he forced himself to stay at the desk making false starts, lest by giving up he should give up forever. For all his books already in print, he might just as well have been the common schoolboy who is told to write of his visit to Aunt Julia and who honestly finds nothing to say except that he arrived on Friday and left on Sunday.

It may be partly because we were all coerced in this fashion that writing on demand comes so hard later on. If so, the old experience contains its own corrective, provided we are willing to look into it, that is to say, look into ourselves. If we ask what is the literary impulse par excellence we are, I think, bound to say that it is a desire to pull together one's conscious self and project it into some tangible constructed thing made up of words and ideas. The written thing may serve ulterior ends, as in exposition or polemic, but its first intention is to transfer a part of our intellectual and emotional insides into an independent and self-sustaining outside. It follows that if we have any doubts about the strength, truth, or beauty of our insides, the doubt acts as an automatic censor which quietly forbids the act of exhibition. Johnny cannot write about the visit to his aunt not merely because he did not initiate the literary idea, but because he feels like a fool relating the trivial things that happen every weekend: "They don't want to hear about that." Generalizing from his dominant conviction, we may say that the antiliterary emotion par excellence is fear. It acts precisely as when one attempts to speak a foreign language; one feels too damn silly for words—and one shuts up.

Obviously, if one were starving or in danger of assault, words would come fast enough, the inner censorship lifted and all sense of affectation gone. This, then, is the desirable situation to create for oneself every morning at nine, or every evening at five. The hopelessly stuck would find it expensive but worth it to hire a gunman to pound on the door and threaten death as a spur to composition. Ideas would come thick and fast and yet be sorted out with wonderful clarity in that final message to one's literary executors.

The sober application of this principle suggests that the writer needs an equivalent of this urgency, this pressure. It cannot help being artificial, like any pulmotoring; but although it need have nothing to do with danger, it must generate some form of excitement. Most of those who have written extensively under varying conditions would say that the true healthful pressure and excitement come from a belief that the things one wants to say form a coherent whole and are in some way needed; that is, the urge is a mixture of the aesthetic and the utilitarian impulses. This seems to be borne out by the observation frequently made that if one can only get something down on paper—anything—one feels no further hindrance to working. The final product may not contain a single sentence of the original, but in the successive drafts one has only a sense of pleasure at molding a resistant lump of clay—cutting away here and adding there in the double light of utility and harmony. It is at the outset, before the matter exists, that the great void paradoxically objectifies one's fear, one's conviction that "they don't want to hear about it."

To know how to begin, then, is the great art—no very profound maxim—but since in any extended piece of work one must begin many times, this is the art which it is essential to master. There is only one way: to study one's needs and quirks, and circumvent one's tricks for escape. The guidebooks will tell you that you should be full of your subject—a very good notion but too abstract. Fullness requires moral and mechanical aids and stout controls. For nothing is more common than to feel a stream of excellent ideas racing past and never a hook to lure them out into the open. This is especially true if one has previously tried to capture them and failed. We may say that our ideas feel like a whole world which is too big and whirling too fast to be pulled out in one piece. True, and this is why first aid at this point consists in not trying to have it born whole. Convince yourself that you are working in clay not marble, on paper not eternal bronze: let that first sentence be as stupid as it wishes. No one will rush out and print it as it stands. Just put it down; then another.[1] Your whole first paragraph or first page may have to be guillotined in any case after your piece is finished: it is a kind of "forebirth." But as modern mathematics has discovered, there can be no second paragraph (which contains your true beginning) until you have a first.

The alternative to beginning stupidly, with a kind of "Er-ah," is to pick out during the earliest mental preparation for the work some idea which will make a good beginning, whether for intrinsic or topical reasons, and let it pull the rest along. Thus I began this essay on the cheering note that those mighty engines, Scott and Dickens, also stalled, and I had this in mind long before I knew what would come next. The danger of this procedure is that a picturesque idea can lead one too far back of the true starting line, and the cleverness or the charm of the idea makes one unwilling to sacrifice it. Burke was rightly accused of beginning every speech by inviting the

1. Another "painful" writer, André Gide, makes the same remark in another way: "Too often I wait for the sentence to finish taking shape in my mind before setting it down. It is better to seize it by the end that first offers itself, head or foot, though not knowing the rest, then pull: the rest will follow along" (*Journal,* 4 June 1930).

Speaker of the House to dance a minuet with him. Ruthless decapitation is the remedy; but note in passing that the error confirms our analysis of the writer's insidious desire to put a cozy padded vest between his tender self and that vague, hostile, roaming animal known as the audience.

Having begun, the writer of even moderate gifts will feel a certain warmth creeping into his veins and rising, as it should, to his head. (In writing, always keep your feet warm, unless you are a full-blooded Indian accustomed to thinking great thoughts while walking barefoot in icy streams.) This genial current, which might prove genius, must be maintained and a physical and mental circulation established, in which blood, ink, and thoughts perform their appointed roles. It is now more than ever important not to let the vigilant censor within freeze everything on a technicality. I refer to that sudden stoppage due to the lack of the right word. Some writers, it is true, are able once started to shape their sentences whole in their heads before putting them down—Gibbon was one of those. But most, I believe, do not. Hence it is fatal for them to feel the entire system of ideas, feelings, and tenuous associations which is now in motion come to a dead stop because some adjective which means "boring" and begins with *n* eludes them. Don't look for it. Leave a blank. The probability is that there is no such word; if there is, it will come up of itself during revision or be rendered unnecessary by it. This sets the rule, by the way, for revision itself: keep going at a reasonable pace to the end, skipping the impossible; then start afresh until you have solved the true problems and removed the insoluble. Remember Barrie's schoolboy who chewed a pencil to splinters and failed the examination because he sought a word halfway between mickle and muckle.

The same law of momentum applies to the search for transitions, to perfecting the rhythm and shape of sentences, even occasionally to the ordering of paragraphs. Don't haggle and fuss but reassure yourself with the knowledge that when you come back to settle these uncertainties and fill these blanks you will still have your mind with you. Especially for young writers who have experienced difficulty and discouragement, the proper aim is that of the learner on the bicycle—keep going, which means a certain speed. Cutting slow capers will come later.

2

More serious than being stopped by a word is the breakdown in ideas. This has to be judged and treated with an even sharper eye for evasion and fraud on the part of the writing self. For the possibilities are several: one is that you have written enough for one day and reached a natural stopping place. It is wise therefore to have not simply a set time for writing—it need not be daily and yet be regular—but also a set "stint" for the day, based on a true, not vainglorious estimate of your powers. Then, when you come to a natural stop somewhere near the set amount, you can knock off with a clear conscience.

Another cause of stoppage is that the work has reached a point of real difficulty—an intellectual decision has to be made, a turning taken, and your mind is balking at it from fatigue or other causes. Or again, it may be that by reason of faulty arrangement there is no obvious bridge from where you are to where you want to go. If the former is true, you must fight it out sooner or later, on the same principles that enabled you to make a beginning. If the latter, devices may help: go back to the beginning, or to some convenient break in the development and read ahead, making but few corrections—just enough to warrant the expense of time and eyesight, but not enough to bog you down. As you approach the halting place, you may suddenly see where you lost the true way and how to bypass the evil spot altogether; or conversely you may find that your fresh running start carries you straight on and over the hump.

Why not an outline? Well, for my taste, outlines are useless, fettering, imbecile. Sometimes, when you get into a state of anarchy, or find yourself writing in circles, it may help to jot down a sketchy outline of the topics (or in a story, of the phases) so far covered. You outline, in short, something that already exists in written form, and this may help to show where you started backstitching. To be sure, a memorandum listing haphazardly what belongs to a particular project is useful. In fact, if you would be a "full" man as you undertake a new piece of work, you should have before you a little stack of slips bearing the ideas that have occurred to you since the subject first came to life in your mind. Otherwise the effort and the sense of treasures just out of reach will be a drain and diversion of writing power. It is jottings of this sort that fill the "Notebooks" at the tail end of "The Works." When I say slips or notebooks, I mean any congenial form of memorandum, for I doubt whether a self-respecting man with a lively flow of ideas can constrain himself to a uniform style and shape of note taking until the sacred fires have begun to cool—say around the age of fifty-one.

In all such matters, I believe in humoring to the greatest extent the timid and stubborn censor which stops work on flimsy pretenses. Grant, by all means, its falsely innocent preferences as to paper, ink, furnishings, and quash its grievances forever. We know that Mark Twain liked to write lying in or on a bed; we know that Schiller needed the smell of apples rotting in his desk. Some like cubicles, others vasty halls. "Writers' requisites," if a Fifth Avenue shop kept them, would astound and demoralize the laity. Historically, they have included silk dressing gowns, cats, horses, pipes, mistresses, particular knickknacks, exotic headgear, currycombs, whips, beverages and drugs, porcelain stoves, and hair shirts. According to one of Bernard De Voto's novels, writing paper of a peculiar blue tint has remarkable properties, about which the author makes an excellent point very subtly: he shows his writer-hero as neurotically exigent on this "trivial" matter, but after we have mocked and put him down as a crank, his work turns out to be a masterpiece. Quite simply, by yielding on such apparently irrational details, the writer is really outwitting his private foe— the excuse-maker within each of us who says: "I can't work today because I haven't any blue paper." Nor is this weakness limited to the literary artist, whether genius or duffer. Before me is a letter just received from a distinguished scientific friend who says: "I have got down to honest work on my article, drawing up elaborate typed notes in what may be a desperate attempt to avoid the actual writing."

That is the true spirit: suspect all out-of-the-way or elaborate preparations. You don't have to sharpen your pencils and sort out paper clips before you begin—unless it be your *regular* warming up. Give yourself no quarter when the temptation strikes, but grab a pen and put down some words—your name even—and a title: something to see, to revise, to carve, to do over in the opposite way. And here comes the advantage of developing a fixation on blue tinted paper. When you have fought and won two or three bloody battles with the insane urge to clean the whole house before making a start, the sight of your favorite implements will speak irresistibly of victory, of accomplishment, of writing done. True, you are at the mercy of the paper mills, as Samuel Butler was the slave of a certain thick book which he used to prop up his writing board at the exact slope of his desire,[2] but such attachments are changeable once they have become a way of tackling work. Even fundamental routines may be recast. I used to wonder how Jane Austen could possibly write in the midst of family conversation, when to me Crusoe's solitude was scarcely adequate. But I learned under necessity to compose (first drafts at least) while keeping a chattering and enterprising child out of mischief in my workroom. The one thing needful is to have an anchorage in some fixed habits and to deal with writer's cowardice precisely as one would with other kinds—facing pain or going over the top. For it is never the specifically literary faculty which balks; it is the affection for one's dear self seeking to protect it against the fearful dangers of laughter, criticism, indifference, and reprints in digest form.

Since habits are rooted in the physical part of us, some writers find it serviceable to begin by doing some act requiring no special thought but which insensibly leads to composition. This doing may be as simple as answering

2. It was Frost's *Lives of Eminent Christians,* as he tells us in "Quis Desiderio?"

correspondence or (with Butler) "posting one's books" —i.e., transcribing notes. But most writers prefer not to spoil the day's freshness by a reminder that relatives exist, nor distract themselves with the scattered subject matter of their notes. The ideal situation perhaps is to awaken with the grand design in mind (it was the last thing thought of before falling asleep), to shave while a matching throng of ideas lathers up within, and to go straight to the blank sheet without exchanging words with anyone.

Here a natural analogy with other arts suggests a few scales and runs on the typewriter, and it may well be that the writer's lack of anything so pleasantly muscular is a real cause of his frequent impotence; even the painter can busy his hands, craftsmanlike. The momentous question behind this comparison is of course the familiar one—pen or typewriter? It is no hedging answer to say, take your choice. But your choice (as I keep repeating) must be thoroughly considered. Is it possible, for instance, that like me you find it discouraging not to see whole paragraphs at a time and not to be able to cross out whole sentences at a time? If so, stick to the pen and use the typewriter to do your first revision as you transcribe. The plastic aspect of written matter is important, and the best revision is undoubtedly made from a clean copy embodying previous revisions. One reason why so much nineteenth-century work is good is that printers' revises were cheap and the writer carved direct on cold print.

Many writers' liking to compose on the typewriter has to do with this clean look of near-print. Hence persons whose fingers are clumsy and whose typed odes are full of fractions and dollar signs should give up the instrument. According to biographers, what they usually take up instead is a short stubby pencil. I do not know why it must be stubby; I mention it only to be fair. Let us by all means have poems, even if written with skewers in goose fat: the point is: Suit Thyself, but pay for it, i.e., *work!*

3

Numberless other facts, tricks, and generalities could be added to this already overlong set of hints. Writers young or old who take an interest in the bare processes of their art (as painters more frequently do) would be well advised to read at large in the considerable literature of exhortation and confession about writing. Ninetenths of it is pedantic or platitudinous, but the other tenth is often amusing and likely to contain particles of illuminating truth, especially if written by a practicing writer. But again, the reader's object being ultimately to make personal applications, he should be on the watch for statements—there must be more than one in the present essay—which make him exclaim: "What an idea! why, it's just the opposite."

The writer must indeed turn everything into grist for *his* mill and no other, as a result of which he acquires both self-knowledge and self-command. His last consideration is therefore his first: what is he afraid of? Only, after he has disciplined himself, he puts the question differently and asks: Whom am I writing for? The century of the common man makes this no easy question to answer, for the common man is a social and political ideal, admirable in the spheres indicated. As a buyer and reader of books he does not exist; one finds humanity instead, which is diverse. One will write for different kinds of people at different times but at any one time there must be some imagined interlocutor, some animated ear trumpet, into which we pour our words. This may be posterity or the children aged eight to ten, but either must be represented in our minds. In judging our own work, we "suit" this mythical person, and our original verdict, "they don't want to hear about that," takes on another meaning—critical yet productive—a kind of ideal collaboration.

This endless conversation in which the writer's censor turns into a helping representative of a given public, is of course most pleasantly realized when the writer has in truth "a reader"—a relative or friend whose judgment he can use. Notice I did not say "whose judgment he will take." For the last step in the writer's liberation through discipline is the discovering of judicial distance —distance from himself, from his work, from his critic, and even from that fickle tiger, his audience.

The practical rules that follow are obvious. Do not read what you have written—much less what you are writing—to whoever will listen; indeed never read unpublished work (except perhaps poems), but give it to be read at leisure. Never show a first draft—except to an old and tried reader who knows from the crude signs what your work may become. Above all, do not talk yourself out of good ideas by trying to expound them to haphazard gatherings. In general, never choose your critic from your immediate family circle: they have usually no knowledge of the processes of writing, however literary they may be as consumers; and in their best-natured act of criticism one may hear the unconscious grinding of axes sounding like a medieval tournament.

No, your special reader (or two or three at most) must be chosen from those who care for writing as much as for you—no writer wants his work to shine in a *charitable* light. And even from your critic-by-appointment you must take only what goes with the grain of your thought and intent. This calls for delicate decisions, since it is always easy to cut off dead tissue and always hard to cut into the living cells that are not true flesh but tumor. The basic principle here as always is to protect the work and not the self.

There is one thing more. A man who writes, as Hardy said, stands up to be shot at, but Hardy was wrong to resent the shooting. So-called established writers who after years of work still wince at criticism are certainly not established in their own souls. Nor does one have to be callous or stubborn about reproof in order to feel solid and to accept one's errors and limitations with a composure which one can then extend to the errors and injustices of critics. Doing so habitually makes one more and more able to *see the work,* which is the prerequisite to producing it, pruning it, and preserving it against the ravages of time.

[1950]

2 English As She's Not Taught

At an educational conference held in Vancouver, leaders of the Canadian school system generally agreed that from half to three-quarters of their students in the first year of college were incompetent in grammar, syntax, and analysis of thought. What was notable in the discussion was that nearly every participant used the English language with uncommon force and precision. Any looseness or jargon heard there came from the three American guests, of whom I was one. Most of our hosts—Canadian teachers, principals, supervisors, and university instructors—had obviously gone through the mill of a classical education; the chairman made a mild pun involving Latin and was rewarded with an immediate laugh. Yet they declared themselves unable to pass on their linguistic accomplishment to the present school generation, and they wanted to know why.

In the United States the same complaint and inquiry has been endemic, commonplace, for quite a while. You come across it in the papers. You hear parents, school people, editors and publishers, lawyers and ministers, men of science and of business, lamenting the fact that their charges or their offspring or their employees can neither spell nor write "decent English." The deplorers blame the modern progressive school or the comics or TV; they feel that in school and outside, something which they call discipline is lacking, and they vaguely connect this lack with a general decline, aggravated by a "crisis." Like everything else, bad English is attributed to our bad times, and the past (which came to an end with the speaker's graduation from college) is credited with one more virtue, that of literary elegance.

The facts seem to me quite different, the causes much more tangled, and the explanation of our linguistic state at once more complex and less vague. For many years now I have been concerned with the art of writing and kept busy at the invidious task of improving other people's utterance, and I cannot see that performance has deteriorated. The level is low but it has not fallen. As a reader of history I am steadily reminded that the writing of any language has always been a hit-and-miss affair. Here is Amos Barrett, our chief source on the battles of Concord and Lexington: "It wont long before their was other minit Compneys . . . We marched Down about a mild or a mild half and we see them acomming . . ." and so on. An illiterate New England farmer? Not so, since he could write; he had been taught and in some way represents "the past." The question he poses is, how do people write who are not professionals or accomplished amateurs? The answer is: badly, at all times.

Writing is at the very least a knack, like drawing or being facile on the piano. Because everybody can speak and form letters, we mistakenly suppose that good, plain, writing is within everybody's power. Would we say this of good, straightforward, accurate drawing? Would we say it of melodic sense and correct, fluent harmonizing at the keyboard? Surely not. We say these are "gifts." Well, so is writing, even the writing of a bread-and-butter note or a simple public notice; and this last suggests that something has happened within the last hundred years to change the relation of the written word to daily life.

Whether it is the records we have to keep in every business and profession or the ceaseless communicating at a distance which modern transport and industry require, the world's work is now unmanageable, unthinkable, without *literature*. Just see how many steps you can take without being confronted with something written or with the necessity of writing something yourself. Having been away for a couple of weeks during the summer, I find a bill from the window washer, who luckily came on a day when the cleaning woman was in the apartment. He has therefore scribbled below the date: "The windows have been cleaned Wed. 12:30 P.M. Your maid was their to verifey the statement"—perfectly clear and adequate. One can even appreciate the change of tense as his mind went from the job just finished to the future when I would be reading this message from the past.

Call this bad writing if you like, it remains perfectly harmless. The danger to the language, if any, does not come from such trifles. It comes rather from the college-bred millions who regularly write and who in the course of their daily work circulate the prevailing mixture of jargon, cant, vogue words, and loose syntax that passes for prose. And the greater part of this verbiage is published, circulated, presumably read. A committee won't sit if its drivelings are not destined for print. Even an interoffice memo goes out in sixteen copies and the schoolchildren's compositions appear verbatim in a mimeographed magazine. Multiply these cultural facts by the huge number of activities which (it would seem) exist only to bombard us with paper, and you have found the source of the belief in a "decline" in writing ability

—no decline at all, simply the infinite duplication of dufferism. This it is which leads us into false comparisons and gloomy thoughts.

2

The apparent deterioration of language is a general phenomenon which is denounced throughout western Europe. One had only to read the catalog of the British Exhibition of 1951 to see the common symptoms in England. Sir Ernest Gowers's excellent little book of a few years earlier, *Plain Words*, was an attempt to cure the universal disease in one congested spot, the civil service, which is presumably the most highly educated professional group in Britain.

In France, the newspapers, the reports of parliamentary debates, and the literary reviews show to what extent ignorance of forms and insensitivity to usage can successfully compete against a training obsessively aimed at verbal competence. And by way of confirmation, M. Jean Delorme, a native observer of the language in French Canada, was led to declare the classic speech "infected" on this side of the Atlantic too. As for Germany, a foreign colleague and correspondent of mine, a person of catholic tastes and broad judgment, volunteers the opinion that "people who cultivate good pure German are nowadays generally unpopular, especially among the devotees of newspaper fiction and articles. The universal barbarism of language has already gone well into the grotesque."

So much for the democratic reality. But great as has been the effect of enlarged "literacy," it does not alone account for what is now seen as linguistic decadence. The educated, in fact the leaders of modern thought, have done as much if not more to confuse the judgment. For what is meant by the misnomer "pure speech" is simply a habit of respect toward usage, which insures a certain fixity in vocabulary, forms, and syntax. Language cannot stand still, but it can change more or less rapidly and violently. During the last hundred years, nearly every intellectual force has worked, in all innocence, against language. The strongest, science and technology, did two damaging things: they poured quantities of awkward new words into the language, and this in turn persuaded everybody that each new thing must have a name, preferably "scientific." These new words, technical or commercial, were fashioned to impress, an air of profundity being imparted by the particularly scientific letters k, x, and o = Kodak, Kleenex, Sapolio. The new technological words that came in were sinful hybrids like "electrocute" and "triphibian," or misunderstood phrases like "personal equation," "nth degree," or "psychological moment"—brain addlers of the greatest potency.

The passion for jargon was soon at its height, from which it shows no sign of descending. Every real or pseudo science pours new verbiage into the street, every separate school or -ism does likewise, without shame or restraint. We can gauge the result from the disapppearance of the dictionary properly so called. Consult what is in many ways the best of them, *Webster's New World Dictionary,* and what you find is a miniature encyclopedia filled with the explanation of initials, proper names, and entries like "macrosporangium" or "abhenry," which are not and never will be words of the English language.

Under the spate of awe-inspiring vocables, the layman naturally feels that he too must dignify his doings and not be left behind in the race for prestige. Common acts must suggest a technical process. Thus we get "contact" and "funnel" as workaday verbs—and "process" itself: "we'll process your application"—as if it were necessary to name the steps or choices of daily life with scientific generality. I know a young businessman who makes jottings of his business thoughts; when he has enough on one topic he *folderizes* them.

What is wrong with all this is not merely that it is new, heedless, vulgar, and unnecessary (all signs of harmful vice in a language) but that jargon swamps thought. The habit of talking through cant words destroys the power of seeing things plain. "I'll contact you to finalize the agreement." What does it mean? The drift is plain enough, but compare: "I'll call at your office to sign the contract." The former raises no clear image or expectation, the latter does. Moreover, the former smells of inflated ego, it fills the mouth in a silly bumptious way.

But who cares? Why fuss?—good questions both. Nobody cares much because we all think it's the deed (or the thing) that counts, not the words. This conviction, too, is a product of modern technology, and its effect is great though unremarked. The power of words over nature, which has played such a role in human history, is now an exploded belief, a dead emotion. Far from words controlling things, it is now things that dictate words. As soon as science was able to chop up the physical world and recombine it in new forms, language followed suit; and this not only among scientists making up new vocables, but among the supposed guardians of the language, the poets and men of letters. It is highly significant that around 1860 writers deliberately began to defy usage and turn syntax upside down. Lewis Carroll and Edward Lear made good fun with it; "obscure" poets such as Rimbaud sought new depths of meaning. There was in this a strong impulse to destroy all convention, for Victorian moralism had made the idea of conventionality at once suspect and hateful. The revolt succeeded and its spirit is still alive; novelty hunting is now a linguistic virtue; or to express it differently, a common influence is at work in Jabberwocky and James Joyce, in the scientist's lingo and in the advertiser's "Dynaflow," "Hydramatic," or "Frigidaire"—which end by becoming household words. In short, modern man is feeling his oats as the manipulator of objects, and he shows it in his manhandling of words.

This helps to explain why the predominant fault of the bad English encountered today is not the crude vulgarism of the untaught but the blithe irresponsibility of the taught. The language is no longer regarded as a common treasure to be hoarded and protected as far as possible. Rather, it is loot from the enemy to be played with, squandered, plastered on for one's adornment. Literary words imperfectly grasped, meanings assumed from bare inspection, monsters spawned for a trivial cause—these are but a few of the signs of squandering. To give examples: the hotel clerk giving me a good room feels bound to mention the well-known person whom "we last hospitalized in that room." Not to lag behind Joyce, the advertiser bids you "slip your feet into these easy-going *leisuals* and breathe a sigh of real comfort."

Undoubtedly these strange desires are often born of the need to ram an idea down unwilling throats. We all fear our neighbor's wandering attention and try to keep him awake by little shocks of singularity, or again by an overdose of meaning. Unfortunately, novelty hunting proceeds from the known to the unknown by a leap of faith. "It was pleasant," writes the author of very workmanlike detective stories, "to watch her face and find his resentment *vitiate* as he made excuses for her."

3

The notable fact is that all this occurs in printed books, written by writers, published (usually) by first-rate firms that employ editors. In speech, the same blunders and distortions come from educated people. It is all very well to say, as one expert has confidently done, that "what certain words really mean is moving toward what they seem to mean," the implication being that after a while everything will be in place. Actually, this leaves meaning nowhere, if only because we're not all moving in step. The *New Yorker* spotted a movie theater sign on which "adultery" was used to mean "adulthood." From an English periodical I learn that some new houses *"affront* the opposite side of the street." If Mrs. Malaprop is going to become the patron saint of English, what is going to prevent "contention" from meaning the same thing as "contentment" or the maker of woodcuts from being called a woodcutter?

There is no getting around it: meaning implies convention, and the discovery that meanings change does not alter the fact that when convention is broken, misunderstanding and chaos are close at hand. True, the vagaries of those who pervert good words to careless misuse seem more often ludicrous than harmful. This might give us comfort if language, like a great maw, could digest anything and dispose of it in time. But language is not a kind of ostrich. Language is alive only by a metaphor drawn from the life of its users. Hence every defect in the language is a defect in somebody.

For language is either the incarnation of our thoughts and feelings or a cloak for their absence. When the ordinary man who has prepared a report on sales up to 30 June rumbles on about "the frame of reference in which the coördination compaign was conceived," he is filling the air with noises, not thoughts.

For self-protection, no doubt, the contemporary mind is opposed to all this quibbling. It speaks with the backing of popular approval when it says: "Stop it! You understand perfectly well what all these people mean. Don't be an old purist looking below the surface and meddling with democratic self-expression." To haggle over language *is* quibbling, of course. All precision is quibbling, whether about decimals in mathematics or grains of drugs in prescriptions—fairly important quibbles. The question is whether in language the results justify the quibble. Well, the public is here the best judge, and it is evident that as a consumer of the written word, the public is always complaining that it cannot understand what it is asked to read: the government blanks, the instructions on the bottle or gadget, the gobbledygook of every trade, the highbrow jargon of the educators, psychiatrists, and social workers, and— one must also add—the prose of literary critics. The great cry today is for improved communication, mass communication, the arts of communication, and yet under the pretext of being free and easy and above quibbling, those who do the most talking and writing indulge themselves in the very obscurities and ambiguities that cause the outcry.

They are abetted, moreover, by another offspring of

the scientific spirit, the professional student of language. In his modern embodiment, the linguist takes the view that whatever occurs in anybody's speech is a fact of language and must not be tampered with, but only caught in flight and pinned on a card. This is "scientific detachment," and it has gone so far that under its influence in many schools all the categories of grammar, syntax, and rhetoric have been discarded. The modern way to learn English or a foreign language is to absorb a phrase-by-phrase enumeration of all that might conceivably be said in ordinary talk—a directory instead of a grammar.

This brings us back to our first difficulty, how to teach the millions the use of their mother tongue *in composition*. We have made nearly everybody literate in the sense of able to read and write words. But that is not writing. Even those who profess disdain for the literary art and the literary quibbles respond automatically to good writing, which they find unexpectedly easy to read and retain, mysteriously "pleasant" as compared with their neighbors' matted prose. The linguists themselves pay lip service to "effective" speech, approving the end while forbidding discrimination among the means.

Now many thousands of people in the United States today exercise this discrimination; there is amid the garbage a steady supply of good writing, modestly done and published—in every newspaper and magazine, over TV and radio, in millions of ads and public notices, in travel booklets, and printed instructions on objects of daily use. Good writing is good writing wherever it occurs, and some of the impugned comics which are supposed to defile the native well of English in our young are far better than acceptable.

It is therefore idle and erroneous to condemn "the

newspapers" or "the radio" en masse. Here too one must discriminate, and the failure to do so is one cause of the trouble—the strange cultural trait whose origin I have sketched and which makes us at once indifferent to our language, full of complaints about it, and irresponsible about mangling it still more. In these conditions people who write well learn to do so by virtue of a strong desire, developed usually under necessity: their job requires lucidity, precision, brevity. If they write advertising copy they must not only make it fit the space but make the words yield the tone.

Tone—that is the starting point of any teaching in composition. What effect are you producing and at what cost of words? The fewer the words, and the more transparent they are, the easier they will be to understand. The closer the ideas they stand for and the more natural their linkage, the more easily will the meaning be retained. Simple in appearance, this formula is yet extremely difficult to apply, and even more arduous to teach. You cannot work on more than one pupil at a time and you must be willing to observe and enter into his mind. On his part, the discipline calls for a thorough immersion in the medium. He must form the habit of attending to words, constructions, accents, and etymologies in everything he reads or hears—just as the painter unceasingly notes line and color and the musician tones. The would-be writer has the harder task because words are entangled with the business of life, and he must stand off from it to look at them, hearing at the same time their harmonies and discords. It is an endless duty, which finally becomes automatic. The ideal writer would mentally recast his own death sentence as he was reading it —if it was a bad sentence.

4

Now such a discipline cannot be imposed from without, and not everybody needs it in full. But its principle, which suffices for ordinary purposes, should be made clear to every beginner, child or adult. Unfortunately, the school system, even when progressive, makes writing an irrational chore approached in the mood of rebellion. The school does this in two ways: by requiring length and by concentrating on correctness. I know very well that correctness was supposedly given up long ago. The modern teacher does not mention it. But if the teacher marks spelling and grammatical errors and speaks of little else, what is a child to think? He gets a mark with the comment "imaginative" or "not imaginative enough" and, most often, "too short," and he is left with no more idea of composition than a cow in a field has of landscape painting. How *does* one judge the right length and get it out of a reluctant brain? Nobody answers, except perhaps with the word "creative," which has brought unmerited gloom to many a cheerful child. Who can be creative on demand, by next Tuesday, and in the requisite amount? In all but a few chatterboxes, mental paralysis is the only result.

Meanwhile the things that are teachable, the ways of translating the flashes of thought into consecutive sentences, are neglected. They have been, most often, neglected in the teachers themselves. How do *they* write or speak, what do *they* read? If they read and write educational literature, as they often must for advancement, are they fit to teach composition? And what of the teachers of other subjects, whose professional jargon also infects their speech—what is their countervailing effect on a child to whom a good English teacher has just imparted a notion of the writer's craft? Suppose the teacher of a course on family life has just been reading *Social Casework* and his mind is irradiated with this: "Familial societality is already a settled question biologically, structured in our inherited bodies and physiology, but the answer to those other questions are not yet safely and irrevocably anatomized." Unless this is immediately thrown up like the nux vomica it is, it will contaminate everybody it touches from pupil to public—in fact the whole blooming familial societality.

The cure is harsh and likely to be unpopular, for it must start with self-denial. It can be initiated by the school but it must not stop there. As many of us as possible must work out of our system, first, all the vogue words that almost always mean nothing but temporary vacancy of mind—such words as "basic," "major," "overall," "personal," "values," "exciting" (everything from a new handbag to a new baby); then all the wormy expressions indicative of bad conscience, false modesty, and genteelism, as in: "Frankly, I don't know too much about it"— a typical formula which tries through candor and whining to minimize ignorance while claiming a kind of merit for it; finally, all the tribal adornments which being cast off may disclose the plain man we would like to be: no frames of reference, field theories, or apperception protocols; no texture, prior to, or in terms of; and the least amount of coordination, dynamics, and concepts.

After the vocabulary has been cleansed, the patient is ready for what our Canadian friends at the Vancouver conference deplored the lack of in the modern undergraduate: analysis of thought. To show what is meant and let criticism begin at home, I choose an example from an educational report entitled "The English Language Arts." It begins: "Because language arts or English is so—" Stop right there! What are language arts?—A perfectly unnecessary phrase of the pseudoscientific kind which tries to "cover." Besides, "language arts or English" is nonsense: ever hear of another language? Moreover, "language arts . . . is" doesn't sound like a happy opening for a report by and to English teachers. Let us go on: English is so what ? Well, "language arts or English is so intimately connected with all knowledge and all living, it is the subject which most often bursts the dikes separating it from others." What do you mean, language is *connected* with living? And how does English connect with *all* knowledge and *all* living? Is the practical knowledge of the Russian engineer intimately connected with English? Do the amoebas speak English? And if this intimacy does exist, then what are these dikes that separate English from other subjects? Are these subjects not part of "all knowledge" with which English is connected—or rather, of which it too is a part?

Cruel work, but necessary if anything akin to thought is to arise from the written word. The Neanderthal glimmer from which the quoted sentence sprang is irrecoverable but its developed form should run something like this: "English, being a medium of communication, cannot be confined within set limits like other subjects; to the peoples whose speech it is, all theoretical knowledge, and indeed most of life, is inseparable from its use."

And this is so true that it justifies the operation just performed on the specimen of nonthought. For although it is possible to think without words and to communicate by signs, our civilization depends, as I said before, on the written word. Writing is embodied thought, and the thought is clear or muddy, graspable or fugitive, according to the purity of the medium. Communication means one thought held in common. What could be more practical than to try making that thought unmistakable?

As for the receiver, the reader, his pleasure or grief is in direct proportion to the pains taken by the writer; to which one can add that the taking of pains brings its special pleasure. I do not mean the satisfaction of vanity, for after a bout of careful writing one is too tired to care; I mean the new perceptions—sensuous or intellectual or comic—to be had all day long in one's encounters with language. Imagine the fun people miss who find nothing remarkable in the sentence (from Sax Rohmer): "The woman's emotions were too tropical for analysis"; or who, trusting too far my disallowance of "contact" as a verb, miss the chance of using it at the hottest, stickiest time of year: "On a day like this, I wouldn't contact anybody for the world."

[1953]

3   A Few Words on a Few Words

Early last spring I received as member of a large and elderly professional association a committee report signed with two names. Each was identified as *Co-chairperson* of the committee. This designation was not new to me, but for some reason the pathos of attaching such a label to live fellow workers struck me with fresh force, and in my sadness I began to reflect on the cause.

Obviously, the reason for using *person* was to avoid *man,* now felt to be the sign of an arrogant imperialism. And in the background, no doubt, was the further wish to get rid of sex reference altogether, to confirm equality by insisting on our common humanness. With that last intention no one will quarrel. The only question is whether it can be served so usefully by terminology that language has to be wrenched out of shape, on top of being misunderstood.

For the pity of the matter is that *man,* in *chairman* and elsewhere, still means *person,* as it does etymologically. As far back as the Sanskrit *manus,* the root *man* means *human being,* with no implication of sex. The German *Mann* and *Mensch,* the Latin *homo* (from which derives the name *human* that we so passionately seek) originally denote the *kind* of creature we all are. *Homo sapiens* means male and female alike. For the male sort, the words were *vir* in Latin, *wer* in Old English (as in *wergeld,* the fine for a crime). *Woman* is the contraction of *wīf-man,* the she-person.

To be sure, confusion set in early, as one would expect, and in the evolution of the Germanic and Romance languages *Mann, Mensch, man, homo, homme,* and *vir,* as well as *wīf, wife, weib,* and *woman,* usurped one or another's place. *Vir*tue, for example, lost its exclusively male tone and became a pre-eminently female attribute. The point to remember is that the meanings switch back and forth, not just one way. In modern German *man sagt,* meaning *they say,* is a common singular for both sexes. In French, the *on* of the corresponding *on dit* is *homo* whittled down and flouting *homme* by meaning either he or she. In English, *man* and *woman* acquired their present differentiation without depriving *man* of its universal, unisex meaning. As an Act of Parliament in 1878 reminded the world in platitudinous terms, "man embraces woman." Unless limited by context, *mankind* means and has always meant humanity entire. It includes the child, who is—in the strict sense of the words— neither man nor woman. Tribal names—Norsemen, Norman, German, Allemand (*Alle Männer*)—are likewise inclusive by their very form.

The present urge to tamper with these familiar notions and nuances is foolishly misdirected. A colleague tells me that he recently gave a new departmental secretary a book note to type, in a great hurry at the end of the day. The young woman was most obliging and pleasant about it and turned out clean copy in a few minutes. My friend took it home to proofread and found it perfect, except for a mysterious gap near the end. A three-letter space had been left after the puzzling word *spokes.* The next day he gingerly asked the girl to explain. She replied quietly that she belonged to a group that had vowed never to type in full the words *chairman, spokesman,* and the like. Does the embargo by these earnest souls extend to *woman?*

No one denies that words are powerful symbols of feeling and attitude and, as such, solid parts of the social structure. That is why from time to time it seems as if to change the structure one need only change the words. The trouble is that the effort can never be thorough and effectual. Language is too subtle, and the force of common speech, set in its course by the generations, sweeps the censor away like a twig in a torrent. Suppose you get rid of *chairman* and *spokesman* by dint of not typing them. What will you do with *fireman, middleman, minute man, Frenchman?* "She phoned and the firepersons came." "Paul Revere was a minute person." Honestly! As for the *Frenchperson,* some fool will want to know whether "it" was a he or a she, while another will mutilate *dragoman,* mistaking it for a native compound with *man* like the rest.

The esthetic sense, not to say the art of literature, is implicated in this silly game. *Person* is not a word to cherish and ubiquitize. Who does not feel that in its most general sense, which asserts anonymity, the word is disagreeably hoity-toity: "There is a person at the door"? In the classic English novel the *young person* holds an ambiguous place—always a she, but now unsavory, now requiring protection. The very etymology of *person* is in doubt, though in mid-career at Rome it certainly had associations with the emptiness of a mask—*persona.* In French, it often means *nobody:* "Who's there?"—*"Personne."* Compare, in American speech, "certain persons believe ..." with the vernacular: "some people think...."

The advertiser's conception of the person ("let us

personalize your paper towels"—as if your initials were your self) is another reason for putting the word in frequent quarantine. Let loose, it tempts to such absurdities as: "I want to enjoy my personal life," "he sold his personal library," and to the appalling compliment: "She's a very real person." In any case, sound and length unsuit it for spontaneous use in dozens of ordinary places: "Yes, the river's dammed; it's a person-made lake." "She had to be personhandled to get her out of the bar."

It is no new discovery that in its ways of distinguishing sex by gender English is capricious and inconvenient. Perhaps it was a good thing to drop the gender of nouns (though reference by pronoun would often benefit from its presence), but it was not sensible to keep gender in the possessives without allowing one of them to indicate either or both sexes indifferently. Just as we miss a *man sagt* or *on dit* and must resort to the plural *they*, so we are commonly driven to: "Has everybody got *their* ticket?" To use *his-or-her* (*her-or-his*) as often as it would be needed in a single sentence or paragraph is quite impracticable.

This is not to say that the use of genders in English has stood still. Notice *it* and *its* in Shakespeare. At some point since Wordsworth wrote "A little child, what should it know of death?" a preference developed for referring to children as he or she—to "personalize" them. And in that same interval we have laudably got rid of *poetess* and *authoress,* as well as of the short-lived *doctress* and *paintress,* which some early feminists demanded as their right. Who will decide whether the road to equality lies through signalizing sex or ignoring it? If credit is to be assigned, then women workers and doers must be readily known by their titles, and *poetess* returns. But if "minority" feeling is to merge in a unified sex psyche, then not even "the way of a man with a maid" will dare be mentioned: the way is the same for both.

In the *person* binge of today this uncertainty remains, for Hannah and Harold still give away the co-chairpersons' sexual identity. Will the next move be toward first names amputated so as to be undetectable, on the model of *Ms?* If English is thus in need of revision and reform (as Strindberg said of the multiplication table) the task ahead is daunting. Will it not be necessary to ostracize *virtue* because of its masculine taint? Will not men denounce the inequity of calling *all* ships "she" and women the injustice of employing the officer known as the "ship's husband"? And what of the naval she which is a *man-of-war? Warperson?*

Nor will it end with the unhappy English tongue. Sex is a source of chaos in language generally, as it is in life. German makes *mädchen* unpardonably neuter, considers *weib* a low word and substitutes *frau,* though it is surely "das ewig-weibliche"—the eternal feminine—that draws us upward (a quite different thing from running after frau or fräulein), to say nothing of the weird form and sense of *frauenzimmer.* In French, *personne* is masculine when it means *nobody* but feminine when it turns around and refers to someone, in which sense it can be applied to a male and then qualified by an adjective in the feminine. A French Communist reminiscing could say: "J'ai rencontré Staline: c'était une personne charmante." Such anomalies abound; they exist in all modern languages as they do in ancient Greek and Latin.

All this insinuates the idea that language cannot be turned at will into a sort of garrulous algebra under the rule of strictness and fixity. Even in algebra one changes the sign, and hence the value, as one moves the terms around. The same adaptability, but far wider, must continue to prevail among words if we are to have a tolerable idiom and the enjoyment that in good hands it can produce. Make childish war on accepted designations, try to force the use of *person* to suppress every hint of sex, and sooner or later free speech will find a way; dire need will inspire dreadful revivals—say, *female* as a noun, in the manner of early nineteenth-century fiction. I see no gain for the lexicon of human dignity either in the prospect of this she-person, with the misleading (fe)*male* at the end and her counterpart "an individual," or in the present peopling of the world with the faceless neuters called *person.*

In short, within the great treasury of terms and their combinations, all of us equal and emancipated human beings must accept the rough with the smooth, the convenient and inconvenient, the direct and roundabout. We must understand that the "brotherhood of man" does not exclude our beloved sisters; that the potent formula Liberty, Equality, Fr—— cannot be revised to end with either Sorority or Personality; that *mankind* in modern usage is not the opposite of *womankind* as *menfolk* is of *womenfolk;* that we are all *fellowman* and *fellowmen* together; and that while *poetess* is offensive and *doctress* ridiculous, *actress* is here to stay.

Even if the banded typists of the world should, to a woman, withhold the last syllable of *spokesman,* their success would hardly legislate the reforms they are after. Important goals must be fought for on their own grounds. Demand equal pay for equal work and the world will come to it. But it was not by the compulsory use of *citoyen* and *citoyenne* after 1789 that democratic manners were established in France. There is more democracy under the Fifth Republic with *monsieur* and *madame* than there was with that affectation under the Committee of Public Safety.

I conclude, on the score of history, etymology, and *Sprachgefühl,* that "Madam chairman" is a correct and decent appellation. No one until recently ever saw in the phrase any paradox, incongruity, or oppugnancy between terms. It is consistent with common sense and perfect equity: the *man* in it denotes either sex, and therefore the key word means precisely *chairperson.* For my part, I shall continue to use it unless stopped by the chair itself, when I will duly defer to authority with the compromise "Madame la Chaise"—this at the risk of being in my turn called Père Lachaise and buried there with full semantic honors.

[1974]

4   Food for the *NRF*

1

I pick up the half-galleys that the publisher has sent me
and start to read. The book is the American edition of
Roger Martin du Gard's *Notes on André Gide*. They
begin, you remember, with the first meeting between
the two men at the offices of the *Nouvelle Revue Fran-
çaise* before the First World War. The translation seems
competent, the atmosphere of forty years ago is well
rendered. But what's this? "On the counter a plateful of
dry buns. . . ." Alas! This must refer to *gâteaux secs* in
the original, and those are cookies, not stale bakery stuff.
Does it matter? Under the eye of eternity, I suppose not.
But right here and now it does. For we are not a mag-
nanimous race, we twentieth centurions. We fasten on
trifles, live on hints, and form conclusions from signs,
which we interpret way beyond the probable. So in a
thousand minds, the *NRF* will be ticketed as a carefree
bohemian place, where the buns of the last monthly
meeting recur until eroded by time; whereas sustained
by Gide's money, the magazine was actually a rather
posh establishment, punctilious in style and proud of
its teas.

I read on and strike other trifles of the same sort. On
a comparative basis, I should still have to call the book
well translated; but drawn off by the act of comparison,
my mind leaves the book and dwells on the theory and
practice of modern translation. I think of the place that

modern French literature occupies in our English-speaking world, and out of thirty years' reading I conjure up the accumulation of hidden error, of factual and emotional misconception, which our awareness and admiration of that literature enshrine.

No doubt the educated American is hardened to the "Frenchy" style of the nineteenth-century classics that one reads in youth—*The Three Musketeers* or *Les Misérables,* in which all colloquialisms of the type *Que voulez-vous?* are given a word-for-word rendering. But doesn't this, combined with the hundreds of unintelligible sentences, lay the foundation for the curious beliefs of adults about France and the French? In some, it is the conviction that life over there is less drab than with us, by virtue of the many provocative turns of thought. In others, it is a faith in the subtlety of every phrase, charged as it obviously is with *hidden* meaning. The philistine, of course, wonders how these foreigners manage to understand one another, and for once he is the better judge, given the evidence presented. Open the latest, "modernized" reissue of *Les Misérables* and you will find, in every other paragraph, sentences such as this one about Napoleon: "He had in his brains the cube of human faculties." Undoubtedly, the routine discredit in which the novels of Victor Hugo now stand owes much to the bald transliteration of a rhetoric which could be out of fashion without seeming insane. As rendered in this same version, Hugo's preface—which is a clear and simple social manifesto—can show only three phrases with a rational meaning. The rest is translator's English.

Scanning the books of our own day, one might think that publishers had acquired a greater sense of responsibility and had recourse for translation to genuine writers, in place of the old-time hack whose livelihood depended on mass output, just as his linguistic knowledge depended on the dictionary he happened to own. This apparent improvement is on the surface only. Enough jokes have been made about the obvious traps for everybody to avoid them. But the same wrong principles prevail as regards the moral and artistic obligations of publisher and translator. It is still taken for granted that literary facility, coupled with what is called a working knowledge of a foreign tongue, is enough to make a translator. Yet this combination of talents, rare as it may be, does not begin to suffice—witness Havelock Ellis, whose version of *Germinal* is made unreadable by gibberish like: "They don't gain enough to live"—meaning *earn* enough to live *on*.

One must go further and say that being an experienced translator is no guarantee of competence in a particular effort, any more than being a concert violinist is a guarantee of a good performance every night. The late C. K. Scott-Moncrieff was perhaps the greatest translator of our century. He gave us a Proust and a Stendhal which, though incomplete, are monuments of an art— triumphs of a type of thought—that I hope to define more fully in a moment. Yet on at least two important occasions he fell from his own high standard and attached his name to the usual illegitimate product in which English and French incestuously mingle. In *Sweet Cheat Gone,* and notably in the dialogue, one is reminded of the Hugo-Dumas school of translators: " 'Listen, first to me,' I replied, 'I don't know what it is, but however astonishing it may be, it cannot be so astonishing as what I have found in my letter. It is a marriage. It is Robert de St. Loup who is marrying Gilberte Swann.' " And even in the narrative parts of the book: "Well, this Albertine so necessary, of love for whom my soul was now almost entirely composed, if Swann had not spoken to me of Balbec, I should never have known her." This sentence is not Proust twisting the tail of syntax, but a common construction that the translator had not only the right but the duty to make readable.

Scott-Moncrieff's other dereliction affects Stendhal. On the title page of the only available edition of *On Love,* our translator is credited with having "directed" the work. This is a solemn responsibility, for the signature is a high guarantee. But the directing cannot have been close or active, for the text abounds in errors and infelicities. Besides gross blunders like "deduct" for "deduce," one meets ambiguities at every turn. According to the preface, for instance, the book "is not a novel and contains none of the distractions of a novel." What Stendhal actually says is that this book will not afford entertainment like a novel. Typical of a still worse incompetence is the rendering of one of the aphorisms at the end: "The majority of men in this world only abandon themselves to their love for a woman after intimacy with her." What the original states is that most *men of the world* only *begin to love,* etc.

When one knows that fifteen years before this luckless attempt upon Stendhal's work a first-rate version by Philip and Cecil N. Sidney Woolf was published here and in England, one begins to imagine an imp of the perverse at work to balk communication between literatures. The truth is that translation is not and has never been recognized as an art—except in the way of lip service. Judges of the art are naturally few, and among its practitioners little or nothing is consciously known of its techniques. Perhaps the decline in classical studies accounts for this deficiency, which should then be called a forgetting of a once established discipline. I remember from my youth a series of trots which were advertised as containing two parallel translations, "the one literal, the other *correct*." Today the distinction would probably puzzle many readers and not a few translators.

In any event, the present oblivion on the part of writers and critics goes with a rooted faith in publishers that translation is a mechanical job, hardly worth paying for, and merely incidental to the finished book. Note how one firm after another will reissue—sometimes at great expense, with illustrations and introductions by good craftsmen—the same execrable translations dating from the Flood. Thus, there is not, I believe, a single readable version of Gautier's *Mademoiselle de Maupin*. When the work was being brought out again in 1943, I offered, as the introducer, to go over the old anonymous text that Tradition and Thrift alike recommended to the publisher. This offer (gratuitous in both senses) was declined with some surprise as surely not worth the time and trouble. My own surprise was that a perfectionist in book production, who did not mean to cheat anybody, should be quite content to palm off a mass of verbiage in the vein of: "His doublet and hose are concealed by aigulets, his gloves smell better than Benjamin. . . . There has sprung up between the planks of the St. Simonian stage a theory of little mushrooms. . . ."

Little mushrooms indeed. Their poison is absorbed into the literary system, which it afflicts with insensitivity to meaning whenever anything foreign—and especially anything French—is concerned. The resulting miscon-

ceptions in turn produce conscious, large-scale misin-
terpretations. For instances of this we need not go much
beyond titles. To be sure, the false lead in a title usually
causes but a passing confusion; one example is Gide's *My
Theatre* for a collection of plays—as if "Shakespeare's
Theatre" meant "Shakespeare's Plays"; another is Stendhal's *Souvenir of Egotism* for "Reminiscences of an Ego-
ist." But in at least one famous instance the established
form of a title is a literary disaster: we all speak of Flaubert's *Sentimental Education*. We do not, it is true, attach
quite the same meaning to "sentimental" here as we do
in Sterne's *Sentimental Journey;* yet unless we are
warned we may miss the fundamental point of the entire
work. The supposition of many an intelligent reader who
knows no French is that the education of Flaubert's hero
was "sentimental" in the sense of nurturing illusions,
fostering "romantic emotions," and that the novel records the consequences. Because he was badly brought
up, Frédéric Moreau lacked the wits to see how "unrealistic" his ideas were—hence his unhappiness, his wander-
ings, and his feeble nostalgia for the youthful days of his
first visit to a house of prostitution.

This interpretation is just tenable enough to prevent
the search for a truer one, and few even of the seekers
would begin by consulting a French dictionary. If they
did they would find that *sentimental(e)* means simply "of
the feelings." Flaubert's title applies not solely to his
hero but to all his characters: he is saying: "Look! This is
how modern life educates the feelings"—the irony rest-
ing on the dreadful word "educates." As to this interpretation of the title there can be no doubt: we have Flaubert's word for it. While at work on the novel, he writes
to a friend: "Je veux faire l'histoire morale des hommes

de ma génération—sentimentale serait plus vrai" (to Mademoiselle de Chantepie, 6 October 1864).

The title once changed, we see that Frédéric is a failure, not because of his emotions of whatever kind, but because of his lack of them. He is not even that sloppy thing *we* call sentimental; he is dry as a bone—and thus only half-brother to Emma Bovary. She at least tried to live out her dreams. She took risks, showed courage, and partly reshaped her surroundings. Her faults of judgment, her "unrealistic" choices are more to be respected than Frédéric's caution and lack of will. Flaubert could and did say that Emma was himself; he never would have owned any kinship, except momentary, with Frédéric. All of which is part of the answer to "What's in a title?"

2

For the translator or would-be translator, Flaubert's misrendered adjective deserves to symbolize Nemesis. Sooner or later he who meddles with foreign texts will succumb to his fate, which is traducing. This may seem a strange necessity, for the criteria of a good translation are few and simple: that it shall be clear to its readers and in keeping with their idiom; that it shall sound like the original author; and that it shall not mislead in substance or implication. But the steps to these results are beyond computing, they are dissimilar in kind, if not contradictory, and they are nowhere codified.

What is easily grasped is that translation requires one to be always in two minds. The act of translating does not consist in carrying words across a no-man's-land, but in answering the question: How would I say this if the notion occurred to me for the first time in my own tongue? Not finding words but turning phrases—hence being sure of what the foreigner thinks and what the native says: two minds with twin thoughts. In moments of fatigue or inattention the performer resumes his more comfortable single mind, and error ensues. From the ignorance which turned *gâteaux secs* into "dry buns" to the awkwardness of Scott-Moncrieff when he nods over Proust's dialogue, the difficulty to be met is that of the schizophrenic: What does this mean? What am I saying? Where is reality in these multitudinous appearances— French, English, adjective, verb, cliché, idiom, plural, inversion, image, illusion, assonance, repetition, brevity, and downright nonsense itself? Translation is not spinning a thread, it is putting a ballet on paper. Sufficient reason—but no excuse—for the inevitable blunder.

The primary danger, illustrated by *sentimental,* is the lure of the homonym. *Contrôler* does not mean "control"; *demander* does not mean "demand"; *un enfant sage* is not a wise child nor a *concurrent* someone who agrees with you. The fact that *diète* does not mean "diet" is annoyingly exemplified by the spoiling of one of Vauvenargues' epigrams in a letter from Matisse to Gertrude Stein. As given in *The Flowers of Friendship,* it reads: "Solitude is to the spirit what diet is to the body." The proper word is of course "fasting." Equally of course, "dieting" sometimes does mean fasting in English and *diète* sometimes does mean "regimen" in French. The lesson is plain: the translator can take nothing for granted. He must be steadily suspicious, inquisitive, a double man vigilant and hostile in self-examination.

Paradoxically, the more at home in each language one feels, the greater the chances of growing blind to gross errors—as I can illustrate from one of mine. It consisted in putting down the English word "dais" for the French *dais*. Now when thinking in English, no other preposition is possible with this noun than "upon"—it is a platform; whereas when thinking in French, sense requires *sous*, i.e., under the canopy. The two languages have each carried off a piece of the ceremonial structure. But in the shuttling state of mind of the translator the difference established by usage disappears in a kind of simultaneous perception which renders the blunder invisible. This cross-eyed condition no doubt accounts also for such a slip as one finds in Mr. Leon Edel's biography of Henry James: "Dressing the balance between remaining abroad and returning home, James etc." Mr. Edel writes and thinks in French as easily as in English and he undoubtedly thought: *dresser le bilan,* but understanding the phrase full well he translated only half of it. In the nature of things, I can only mention, not specify, other types of blunder that, like everybody else, I must have made in the course of scholarly work, when translating from languages that one can read and "understand," but that one will never know as strictly as one must in order to put oneself forward as a translator.

Blindness being the fundamental, hidden, and recurring difficulty, it must be consciously and perpetually guarded against. Fortunately there are tricks and tools that the careful workman can use. One obvious device is to lay aside the first draft of the translation until the original has faded from the mind, and to take it up for revision by itself, quite as if it were an original composition. It is easy then to catch some of the unnatural turns. But the laying aside requires time, for the primary idiom lingers in the memory an astonishingly long while and, reviving at sight of the equivalent, makes deceptively meaningful whole sentences that are in fact senseless to the monolingual reader for whom they are intended. Many translators cannot afford the pause; others, as they have told me, do not recognize the need. They work as it were always in the teeth of the original and think they are thereby insuring fidelity. It is painful to reflect that we may owe to this misguided zeal the faults that mar most of Croce's works in English and many a dubious passage in the devoted rendering of Gide's *Journal*—four volumes which will not soon be done again, but in which we read, for example, that a play of Molière's ends "atrociously" when Gide means "cruelly" (*atrocement*); and in which the purity of style the author prized so highly is blemished by continual lapses from idiom: "It is not one of the least interests of this book," etc.

A second point of method for the translator is to bring to consciousness all the differences of form, rhythm, sense, and habit that he can find between his two languages. (I assume that no translator other than a hack or a genius will attempt more than two, and to simplify discourse I shall continue to generalize from the experience of turning French into English.) Any published translator will tell you how difficult it is to find steady English equivalents for *esprit, constater, il s'agit de*, etc., but few seem to know that there are aids to reflection on these matters. It is a sign of the unprofessional character of the business that no translator with whom I have talked had ever heard of *Les faux amis* by Koessler and Derocquigny or *Le mot juste* by J. G. Anderson (rev. Harmer). Both books list and define words that look alike but mean different things in French and English. The former, which is especially rich in comment and examples, works from the French side upon English words; the latter confronts kindred pairs of words and idioms in a spirit of enlightened neutrality. Both should be not merely consulted at need, but read and reread (occasionally corrected) until the chief oddities of both tongues have become items of familiar knowledge—like the fact that a meter is not the same as a yard.

This suggests the next step. Grim as it may sound, the translator must keep in training by asking himself, at any time, while reading any book (in either language): How would I say it in English? (in French?) Like the violinist, he is an interpreter and cannot avoid thoughts of adroit fingering even in the midst of pleasure. Indeed, the translator cannot help becoming something of a grammarian in the unfavorable sense: he is bound to be a reader of grammars and dictionaries.

No one volume is perfect enough for his needs, though it may be said that the professional must own at least Grevisse, *Le bon usage* (the counterpart of Fowler's *Modern English Usage*), and should have access to Littré. Of lesser dictionaries, the Oxford French is remarkably compact and true, and it begins with a soundly philosophic preface on the kind of life one must lead in order to give accurate renderings: not by any means a description of the Good Life, but rather of the full life, poised between literature and worldly pursuits, and dedicated to matching words with all men on all occasions. The compilers themselves answer to these specifications, even though they too stumble once or twice: they will tell you that *jeu d'esprit* means witticism, which it doesn't.

Every turn of the road brings us face to face with Nemesis, that is to say, with the recognition that complete and unfailing equivalence is impossible. Accordingly the third duty of the translator is to atone for inevitable shortcomings by a sustained impersonation of his original. He may rob Peter by reflex action but he pays Paul with compound interest. He strives, that is, to bring his text into spiritual conformity with that of his author. To do this with any success is as much the fruit of technique as of inspiration—the technique of writing English no less than that of understanding French. For I posit that a good translation is addressed to living readers and dare not be an exercise in archaism. At every point, then, the translator must gauge the force and function of the elements before him and make sure that no force is lost, no function forgotten. The sums and products must balance.

Force may be easy to weigh and hard to reproduce. In translating Diderot's *Rameau's Nephew,* I discovered that terms of contempt or abuse are of a discouraging specificity: any given term implies so much and no more, and its nearest English equivalent always hits above or below the mark. The dictionary meaning, therefore, hardly enters into the equation. Rather, one is paralyzed by the very aptness of the term. The problem is to recapture this felicity with the vocabulary available now, a hundred and fifty years later: were there "crooks" in the eighteenth century? Surely there are no "rogues" now, and even "scoundrels" are on the wane. Dictionaries fail here because language itself breaks down.

As for the function of the given phrase, sentence, paragraph, it can be fully understood and properly rendered only if one has an inkling of what the author could have written in its place had he been so minded—other words and even other ideas. To know or guess these possibilities calls for familiarity with the author and his tradition. It is not too much to say that to translate a work of any intellectual and literary pretensions requires a sympathetic knowledge of the whole canon. How far "the canon" extends is a matter to be determined in each attempt.

For a good many years I had toyed with the idea of putting Flaubert's *Dictionnaire des idées reçues* into English, and in moments of leisure I had filled a notebook with scraps of those terse and baffling definitions. Sooner or later, I knew, a call to complete the job would come, whether from on high or from a publisher. I dreaded the day, for I knew the difficulties by heart, or more exactly, the dilemmas. I had as many as three and four versions of the problematic items and secretly hankered to give them all—escape per variorum. The call came, at once from on high and from a publisher, whose editor showed me in a copy of *Gentry* the translation of a few excerpts from the *Dictionnaire* and extended an invitation to do the whole.

The published fragment showed an enviable courage and was not without merit, though it contained some easily avoidable errors. To call political economy "a science without guts" (instead of "heartless") and to confuse "parents" with "relatives" when the injunction was to avoid seeing them, suggested a newcomer to the craft of translating, if not to Flaubert. I began to sort my notes, ponder the title, and (to lessen my own fallibility) I started rereading *Bouvard et Pécuchet,* the Correspondence, the works of Descharmes, Steegmuller, Dumesnil and others, not excluding good old Tarver (*Life and Letters of Flaubert*), despite his penchant for what I have called "translator's English."

When it came to getting the Dictionary down on paper, the particular problems had fused into the general one of how often to take liberties. They had to be frequent and great because the book itself is a sort of bare exhibition of stupidity, without internal or external commentary. Each definition is like a biologist's slide: to see the point of it one must know what was in the observer's mind when he prepared it. The French reader has trouble too, though less, because he can often compare what he expects with what the definition leaves out. The translation must therefore supply (or substitute) a context not found within the original, and at the same time keep matching its brevity and commonplaceness. No one could hope to win every trick of such a game. Add to this challenge Flaubert's extravagant playing on words, allusions, and ideas, and anyone will concede the right to transmute as a means to translating. A simple case is that of *message*—"nobler than 'letter'" says Flaubert. True in French but certainly not in English. Obviously what is wanted is "missive." For the same reason, modified by others, *banquet* must become "reunion"; *coup de Jarnac,* "Parthian shot"; and *folliculaire,* "newshound." The ultimate question was whether *Idées reçues* in the title should or should not be rendered as "Received Ideas." The term certainly exists in English; almost every dictionary records it in the desired sense. But it somehow needs surrounding matter to be perfectly clear: it will not do in a title; it has to be: *Accepted Ideas.*

Entrenched behind isolated words and phrases, the literalist may carp at this and other decisions. There are two schools of thought about translation, and the professional worker should read the arguments of Tytler, Postgate, Rudler, Belloc, and the rest. For my part, I side with those who maintain that not poetry alone but even the flattest of flat prose consists of words plus echoes. Some of these echoes are fixed (and recognized) in idioms, cliches, and dead metaphors; others exist more vagrantly, in literature, in capricious habit, sometimes in mere sounds. For example, the young Berlioz writes to his father that a piece of music was thirty times more impressive than he expected. Who does not feel at once that in English "thirty" is all wrong? It suggests an exact measurement, our ears demand the familiar "fifty times." To make thirty equal fifty is therefore to translate more exactly, not less.

If this rule is ill-observed, it is perhaps because carrying it out would demand encyclopedic experience and attention. Nothing is more difficult than to keep abreast, in two languages, of the ceaseless variations of rank, color, and popularity within the vocabulary. To take a trivial instance, how could a nonresident foreigner learn that in American English the simple word "appliance" is almost never spoken though it appears on nearly every hardware shop and the letterheads of countless manufacturers? Out of such minutiae arise the differences between Britain's English and ours—differences which, as they affect literature, have been charted by Mr. G. V. Carey in his little book, *American into English*. How much more profound and harder to chart the differences between languages that are only cognate, and that keep shifting independently, with no contacts save through translators themselves!

3

From here on the consideration of linguistic detail merges with the great questions of cultural exchange, political friction, and popular superstition. The unsophisticated American returns from his first trip abroad convinced that the entire French people is touched with philosophy and hourly inspired to the picturesque because the common folk use such delightful latinized expressions. In reverse, I have listened to a demonstration showing that the phrase "How do you do" could only become current among such practical peoples as the Anglo-Saxon, illogical but eager for know-how even while shaking hands.

One aspect, certainly, of international communication is far from a joke. It is to find and train high-grade translators. At a time when some 950 world organizations are trying to tie threads of discourse instead of snapping them, we should be seeing the rise of an ethics of translation, or at least a set of first principles by which to gauge competence. We see nothing of the kind, but rather an increase (by volume) of irresponsible practices. I have had occasion to read quite closely two of the quarterlies—one private, the other official—that publish in more than one language. Both of them are edited by conscientious people who do their best to produce valid reading matter. But the available translators are simply not equal to the task or not willing to discharge it honestly. From one issue that I read in copy form, it was clear that the French translators had barely revised their first typed draft. Each page contained dozens of errors of the grossest kind—not only misrepresentations of the meaning, but errors in French, as if a foreign author scarcely deserved to appear in decent style. I was assured that all these paid perverters were completely *bilingues;* all one could reply was that if so their speech was the new *bilinguesgate,* a reproach to the users and to their upbringing.

In the other, the official quarterly, a greater effort is made to understand each author and recast his thought in idiomatic form. Yet a comparison of original and translation (which are printed side by side) usually shows how frequently main points escape the hasty converter. In an article by Mr. Peter Ustinov, precisely on translations for the stage, the well-known playwright refers to the strength a writer wields when "entrenched in the sinews of his native language." The key phrase, which is perhaps strained but not unreasonable in its metaphor, becomes in French "entering the sinuosities." Mr. Ustinov goes on: "The French language seems to me the very antithesis of the English. It is accurate, hard, polished, although it contrives, by the very beauty of its music, to cement the sparkling sentences with words of sensuous languor." In translation, the last clause reads: "even though it compels you, for the sake of beauty, to cement," etc.—which is sheer nonsense.

The theater being a popular and socially responsive art, it should seem important to have foreign plays accurately transported across frontiers. The whole purpose of adaptation is to enable the audience to grasp at once how life is lived—wherever it may be. Yet in the verbal part, which is surely the most manageable, good adaptations are rare. Mr. Eric Bentley, who collects them for his volumes *From the Modern Repertory,* tells me that it is difficult to find texts that can be relied on throughout. The simple requirements of sayability, sense, and truth to the original seldom come together. From my own knowledge I can testify that it passes belief what the French listen to and read as the works of Bernard Shaw. The title of *The Apple Cart (La charrette aux pommes)* indicates how the rest goes—blind man's buff amid strange idioms. Every speech suggests the plight of the indifferent pupil who excuses himself with a stubborn "That's what it says." The pity is that the idioms in Shaw are quite translatable and the apple cart image too: the French for it is *renverser le pot de fleurs.*

At the opera, of course, sound and meaning fare still worse. After repeated efforts, one can point only to Edward Dent's versions of the Mozart librettos as successes in the genre. If we listen on other occasions, say to *Boris Godunov,* we are punished by hearing about vi*lá*gers and monk*eree.* The old texts, full of 'neath and 'gainst, have no doubt been discarded as the silly nonsense they were, but the modern substitutes are either hard to sing or deplorably prosaic: in a recent version of Monteverdi, his music is made to accompany suburban-train diction. It becomes a mercy that enunciation in singers is still as rudimentary as notions of fitness among musical translators.

All these signs of primitivism in one important department of our culture point in the same direction. They point to the need for a new discipline, perhaps a new institution. If we take our century at its word, it is pining for Communication. It believes in the Communication Arts and has got as far as inventing the dismal phrase. Unesco takes one shaky step farther and issues "bilingual" cards headed, on one side, *Department de l'Information* and on the other, "Department of Mass Communication." Well, our century and Unesco and any other massive communicators might do worse (by which I mean they could not do better) than to set up an Institute of Translation.

Its purpose would be, first, to collect a library of works of theory and reference—a bigger task than it may seem if one forgets the technological, legal, medical, and other special vocabularies that "culture" now draws on, and the innumerable languages that the world now recognizes. The institute's next duty would be to elaborate canons, appoint a teaching staff, prepare manuals, and devise a curriculum. When properly equipped, like any other school, it could accept students, train them, and finally certify them, both at large and for specified languages. The staff, aided by graduates returning for advanced study, would in time be expected to produce the handbooks and lexicons that are still wanting, and perhaps to exert a steadily increasing critical pressure on those who write and publish.

Meanwhile, every reader of translated matter must continue to be on his guard. It will not do to think that grave misunderstandings occur only as isolated and dramatic events, like the one Churchill reports in his war book, when the verb "to table" a suggestion, meaning opposite things to the group, nearly split an Anglo-American military council. Nor is it only the Japanese language, with its surfeit of homonyms, which runs the risk of fatal ambiguity, as in the famous "Mokusatsu Mistake." The passage from one tongue to another always entails danger, even in a library, even in a bank—as I recently discovered from a friend's inquiry: Didn't *en provenance des Etats-Unis* applied to goods mean "originating in the United States"? This ancient firm had always assumed that it did, but now a question had arisen. Very properly, too, I had to admit, since the French phrase implies nothing about origin; all it says is "coming from." Yet *provenance* by itself, in both languages, commonly suggests an ultimate source. This is but another proof of the generality that all translation depends on verbal tact, and that consequently no such thing as an IBM translating machine is possible: it would be as unsatisfactory as what we now have.

When I am tempted to console myself with the thought that things *cannot* be as bad as I make out, that I must see trouble magnified from being too close to it, I take down from the shelf a volume from a respectable encyclopedia which, until a recent revision, thirty years overdue, included translated articles by foreign authorities. Those on French art and letters addressed the students thus: "The reverie, face to face with wide horizons, serene and tender piety, sometimes even a real gladness, are blended in those accents, the character of which, well defined, remains as striking as in former times." One dare not assume that the secret of such prose has been lost. It was only a few months ago that the English edition of Simone de Beauvoir's book about the United States added to her grievous misconceptions about this country no less grievous misreadings of her text. We could all smile and make the mental correction when we read there that Gerhardt Eisler was indicted for conspiracy, falsifying passports, and "despising Congress"; we recognized translator's English in quaint asides like "Thirty-six hours in Chicago, this was little"; but there was no way of guessing the author's mind from misconstrued tenses and wrong words. Here was an American speaking to Madame de Beauvoir: "If everyone had good faith, all would be well; and he added forcefully, '*All* would be well.' " This stood for: " 'If everyone showed a little good will ['was cooperative' is what I bet he said] things would go all right,' said he cheerfully. And he added with spirit: 'Things *will* go all right.' "

I have not said anything about translating poetry, a distinct problem about which [the late] Dudley Fitts, a translator of the first rank, made frequent comments in book reviews. He should theorize at greater length for the benefit of the future institute, even though verse translators seldom fail from haste or indifference, and are perhaps not greatly improvable by instruction. Indeed, Father Ronald Knox's excellent little book *On Englishing the Bible* would lead one to conclude that in poetical and spiritual matters a good many readers prefer gibberish and contortions to simplicity and sense. And it could be argued that if the Western world has survived the dire mistranslations of the Bible it can survive anything. Are we then to be forced at last to the conclusion that a rough approximation of anyone's meaning, that of the saints and the prophets included, is quite good enough for a busy world? This might be the reason why translators are "a dispirited race," as Francis Steegmuller once called them. Were one driven to believe this, the temptation would be great to retire from the intellectual scene altogether; retire on a *diète* of dry buns and beat one's breast with loud lament, or as we say in English, pushing the cries of a desesperate.

[1953]

Writers and Editors

5   Lincoln the Writer

A great man of the past is hard to know, because his legend, which is a sort of friendly caricature, hides him like a disguise. He is one thing to the man in the street and another to those who study him closely—and who seldom agree. And when a man is so great that not one but half a dozen legends are familiar to all who recognize his name, he becomes once more a mystery, almost as if he were an unknown.

This is the situation that Lincoln occupies in the United States on the 150th anniversary of his birth. Everybody knows who he was and what he did. But what was he like? For most people, Lincoln remains the rail splitter, the shrewd country lawyer, the cracker-barrel philosopher and humorist, the statesman who saved the Union, and the compassionate leader who saved many a soldier from death by court-martial, only to meet his own end as a martyr.

Not being a Lincoln scholar, I have no wish to deal with any of these images of Lincoln. I want only to help celebrate his sesquicentennial year by bringing out a Lincoln who I am sure is real though unseen. The Lincoln I know and revere is a historical figure who should stand—I will not say, instead of, but by the side of all the others. No one need forget the golden legends, yet anyone may find it rewarding to move them aside a little so as to get a glimpse of the unsuspected Lincoln I have so vividly in mind.

I refer to Lincoln the artist, the maker of a style that is unique in English prose and doubly astonishing in the history of American literature, for nothing led up to it. The Lincoln who speaks to me through the written word is a figure no longer to be described wholly or mainly by the old adjectives, shrewd, humorous, or saintly, but rather as one combining the traits that biography reports in certain artists among the greatest—passionate, gloomy, seeming-cold, and conscious of superiority.

These elements in Lincoln's makeup have been noticed before, but they take on a new meaning in the light of the new motive I detect in his prose. For his style, the plain, undecorated language in which he addresses posterity, is no mere knack with words. It is the manifestation of a mode of thought, of an outlook which colors every act of the writer's and tells us how he rated life. Only let his choice of words, the rhythm and shape of his utterances, linger in the ear, and you begin to feel as he did—hence to discern unplumbed depths in the quiet intent of a conscious artist.

But before taking this path of discovery, it is necessary to dispose of a few too familiar ideas. The first is that we already know all there is to know about Lincoln's prose. Does not every schoolchild learn that the Gettysburg Address is beautiful, hearing this said so often that he ends by believing it? The belief is general, of course, but come by in this way, it is not worth much. One proof of its little meaning is that most Americans also believe that for fifty years Lincoln's connection with the literary art was to tell racy stories. Then, suddenly, on a train journey to Gettysburg he wrote a masterpiece. This is not the way great artists go to work—so obviously not, that to speak of Lincoln as an *artist* will probably strike some readers as a paradox or a joke. Even so, the puzzle remains: How did this strange man from Illinois produce, not a few happy phrases, but an unmistakable style?

On this point the books by experts do no better than the public. The latest collective attempt to write a literary history of the United States does indeed speak of Lincoln's styles, in the plural: but this reference is really to Lincoln's various tones, ranging from the familiar to the elevated. Like all other books that I have searched through, this authoritative work always talks of the subject or the occasion of Lincoln's words when attempting to explain the power of his best-known pieces. It is as if a painter's genius were explained by the landscapes he depicted.

Lincoln has indeed had praise as a writer, but nearly all of it has been conventional and absentminded. The few authors of serious studies have fallen into sentimentality and incoherence. Thus, in the Hay and Nicolay edition of Lincoln's works, a famous editor of the nineties writes: "Of style, in the ordinary use of the word, Lincoln may be said to have had little. There was nothing ambitiously elaborate or self-consciously simple in Lincoln's way of writing. He had not the scholar's range of words. He was not always grammatically accurate. He would doubtless have been very much surprised if anyone had told him that he 'had' a style at all."

Here one feels like asking: Then why discuss "Lincoln as a writer"? The answer is unconvincing: "And yet, because he was determined to be understood, because he was honest, because he had a warm and true heart, because he had read good books eagerly and not coldly, and because there was in him a native good taste, as well as a strain of imagination, he achieved a singularly clear and forcible style, which took color from his own noble character and became a thing individual and distinguished...."

So the man who had no style had a style—clear, forcible, individual and distinguished. This is as odd a piece of reasoning as that offered by the late Senator Beveridge: "The cold fact is that not one faint glimmer appears in his whole life, at least before his Cooper Union speech, which so much as suggests the radiance of the last two years." Perhaps a senator is never a good judge of what a president writes: this one asks us to believe in a miracle. One would think the "serious" critics had simply failed to read their author.

Yet they must have read him, to be so obviously bothered. "How did he do it?" they wonder. They think of the momentous issues of the Civil War, of the grueling four years in Washington, of the man beset by politicians who were too aggressive and by generals who were not enough so, and the solution flashes upon them: "It was the strain that turned homespun into great literature." This is again to confuse a literary occasion with the literary power which rises to it. The famous documents—the two inaugurals, the Gettysburg Address, the letter to Mrs. Bixby—marvelous as they are, do not solve the riddle. On the contrary, the subjects have such a grip on our emotions that we begin to think almost anybody could have moved us. For all these reasons—inadequate criticism, overfamiliarity with a few masterpieces, ignorance of Lincoln's early work and the consequent suppression of

Lincoln the Writer   69

one whole side of his character—we must go back to the source and begin at the beginning.

Pick up any early volume of Lincoln's works and start reading as if you were approaching a new author. Pretend you know none of the anecdotes, nothing of the way the story embedded in these pages comes out. Your aim is to see a life unfold and to descry the character of the man from his own words, written, most of them, not to be published, but to be felt.

Here is Lincoln at twenty-three telling the people of his district by means of a handbill that they should send him to the state legislature: "Upon the subjects of which I have treated, I have spoken as I thought. I may be wrong in regard to any or all of them; but holding it a sound maxim that it is better to be only sometimes right than at all times wrong, so soon as I discover my opinions to be erroneous, I shall be ready to renounce them." And he closes his appeal for votes on an unpolitical note suggestive of melancholy thoughts: "But if the good people in their wisdom shall see fit to keep me in the background, I have been too familiar with disappointments to be very much chagrined."

One does not need to be a literary man to see that Lincoln was a born writer, nor a psychologist to guess that here is a youth of uncommon mold—strangely self-assertive, yet detached, and also laboring under a sense of misfortune.

For his handbill Lincoln may have had to seek help with his spelling, which was always uncertain, but the rhythm of those sentences was never taught by a grammar book. Lincoln, as he himself said, went to school "by littles," which did not in the aggregate amount to a year.

Everybody remembers the story of his reading the Bible in the light of the fire and scribbling with charcoal on the back of the shovel. But millions have read the Bible and not become even passable writers. The neglected truth is that not one but several persons who remembered his childhood remarked on the boy's singular determination to express his thoughts in the best way.

His stepmother gave an account of the boy which prefigures the literary artist much more than the rail splitter: "He didn't like physical labor. He read all the books he could lay his hands on. . . . When he came across a passage that struck him, he would write it down on boards if he had no paper and keep it there till he did get paper, then he would rewrite it, look at it, repeat it." Later, Lincoln's law partner, William H. Herndon, recorded the persistence of this obsessive habit with words: "He used to bore me terribly by his methods. . . . Mr. Lincoln would doubly explain things to me that needed no explanation. . . . Mr. Lincoln was a very patient man generally, but . . . just go at Lincoln with abstractions, glittering generalities, indefiniteness, mistiness of idea or expression. Here he flew up and became vexed, and sometimes foolishly so."

In youth, Lincoln had tried to be a poet, but found he lacked the gift. What he could do was think with complete clarity in words and imagine the workings of others' minds at the same time. One does not read far in his works before discovering that as a writer he toiled above all to find the true order for his thoughts—order first, and then a lightninglike brevity. Here is how he writes in 1846, a young politician far from the limelight, and of whom no one expected a lapidary style: "If I falsify in this you can convict me. The witnesses live, and can tell." There is a fire in this, and a control of it, which shows the master.

That control of words implied a corresponding control of the emotions. Herndon described several times in his lectures and papers the eccentric temperament of his lifelong partner. This portrait the kindly sentimental people have not been willing to accept. But Herndon's sense of greatness was finer than that of the admirers from afar, who worship rather storybook heroes than the mysterious, difficult, unsatisfactory sort of great man—the only sort that history provides.

What did Herndon say? He said that Lincoln was a man of sudden and violent moods, often plunged in deathly melancholy for hours, then suddenly lively and ready to joke; that Lincoln was self-centered and cold, not given to revealing his plans or opinions, and ruthless in using others' help and influence; that Lincoln was idle for long stretches of time, during which he read newspapers or simply brooded; that Lincoln had a disconcerting power to see into questions, events, and persons, never deceived by their incidental features or conventional garb, but extracting the central matter as one cores an apple; that Lincoln was a man of strong passions and mystical longings, which he repressed because his mind showed him their futility, and that this made him cold-blooded and a fatalist.

In addition, as we know from other sources, Lincoln was subject to vague fears and dark superstitions. Strange episodes, though few, marked his relations with women, including his wife-to-be, Mary Todd. He was subject, as some of his verses show, to obsessional gloom about separation, insanity, and death. We should bear in mind that Lincoln was orphaned, reared by a stepmother, and early cast adrift to make his own way. His strangely detached attitude toward himself, his premonitions and depressions, his morbid regard for truth and abnormal suppression of aggressive impulses, suggest that he hugged a secret wound which ultimately made out of an apparent common man the unique figure of an artist-saint.

Lincoln moreover believed that his mother was the illegitimate daughter of a Virginia planter, and like others who have known or fancied themselves of irregular descent, he had a powerful, unreasoned faith in his own destiny—a destiny he felt would combine greatness and disaster.

Whatever psychiatry might say to this, criticism recognizes the traits of a type of artist one might call "the dark outcast." Michelangelo and Byron come to mind as examples. In such men the sense of isolation from others is in the emotions alone. The mind remains a clear and fine instrument of common sense—Michelangelo built buildings, and Byron brilliantly organized the Greeks in their revolt against Turkey. In Lincoln there is no incompatibility between the lawyer-statesman, whom we all know, and the artist, whose physiognomy I have been trying to sketch.

Lincoln's detachment was what produced his mastery over men. Had he not, as president, towered in mind and will over his cabinet, they would have crushed or used him without remorse. Chase, Seward, Stanton, the Blairs, McClellan had among them enough egotism and ability to wreck several administrations. Each thought Lincoln would be an easy victim. It was not until he was removed from their midst that any of them conceived of him as an apparition greater than themselves. During his life their dominant feeling was exasperation with him for making them feel baffled. They could not bring him down to their reach. John Hay, who saw the long struggle, confirms Herndon's judgments: "It is absurd to call him a modest man. No great man was ever modest. It was his intellectual arrogance and unconscious assumption of superiority that men like Chase and Sumner could never forgive."

This is a different Lincoln from the clumsy country lawyer who makes no great pretensions, but has a trick or two up his sleeve and wins the day for righteousness because his heart is pure. Lincoln's purity was that of a supremely conscious genius, not of an innocent. And if we ask what kind of genius enables a man to master a new and sophisticated scene as Lincoln did, without the aid of what are called personal advantages, with little experience in affairs of state and no established following, the the answer is: military genius or its close kin, artistic genius.

The artist contrives means and marshals forces that the beholder takes for granted and that the bungler never discovers for himself. The artist is always scheming to conquer his material and his audience. When we speak of his craft, we mean quite literally that he is crafty.

Lincoln acquired his power over words in the only two ways known to man—by reading and by writing. His reading was small in range and much of a kind: the Bible, Bunyan, Byron, Burns, Defoe, Shakespeare, and a then-current edition of Aesop's Fables. These are books from which a genius would extract the lesson of terseness and strength. The Bible and Shakespeare's poetry would be less influential than Shakespeare's prose, whose rapid twists and turns Lincoln often rivals, though without imagery. The four other British writers are all devotees of the telling phrase, rather than the suggestive. As for Aesop, the similarity of his stories with the anecdotes Lincoln liked to tell—always in the same words—is obvious. But another parallel occurs, that between the shortness of a fable and the mania Lincoln had for condensing any matter into the fewest words:

"John Fitzgerald, eighteen years of age, able-bodied, but without pecuniary means, came directly from Ireland to Springfield, Illinois, and there stopped, and sought employment, with no present intention of returning to Ireland or going elsewhere. After remaining in the city some three weeks, part of the time employed, and part not, he fell sick, and became a public charge. It has been submitted to me, whether the City of Springfield, or the County of Sangamon is, by law, to bear the charge."

As Lincoln himself wrote on another occasion, "This is not a long letter, but it contains the whole story." And the paragraph would prove, if it were necessary, that style is independent of attractive subject matter. The pleasure it gives is that of lucidity and motion, the motion of Lincoln's mind.

In his own day, Lincoln's prose was found flat, dull, lacking in taste. It differed radically in form and tone from the accepted models—Webster's or Channing's for speeches, Bryant's or Greeley's for journalism. Once or twice, Lincoln did imitate their genteel circumlocutions or resonant abstractions. But these were exercises he never repeated. His style, well in hand by his thirtieth year and richly developed by his fiftieth, has the eloquence which comes of the contrast between transparency of medium and density of thought. Consider this episode from a lyceum lecture written when Lincoln was twenty-nine:

"Turn, then, to that horror-striking scene at St. Louis. A single victim was only sacrificed there. His story is very short; and is, perhaps, the most highly tragic of anything of its length that has ever been witnessed in real life. A mulatto man by the name of McIntosh was seized in the street, dragged to the suburbs of the city, chained to a tree, and actually burned to death; and all within a single hour from the time he had been a freeman, attending to his own business, and at peace with the world."

Notice the contrasting rhythm of the two sentences: "A single victim was only sacrificed there. His story is very short." The sentences are very short, too, but let anyone try imitating their continuous flow or subdued emotion on the characteristic Lincolnian theme of the swift passage from the business of life to death.

Lincoln's prose works fall into three categories: speeches, letters, and proclamations. The speeches range from legal briefs and arguments to political debates. The proclamations begin with his first offer of his services as a public servant and end with his presidential statements of policy or calls to Thanksgiving between 1861 and 1865. The letters naturally cover his life span and a great diversity of subjects. They are, I surmise, the crucible in which Lincoln cast his style. By the time he was in the White House, he could frame, impromptu, hundreds of messages such as this telegram to General McClellan: "I have just read your despatch about sore-tongued and fatigued horses. Will you pardon me for asking what the horses of your army have done since the battle of Antietam that fatigues anything?"

Something of Lincoln's tone obviously comes from the practice of legal thought. It would be surprising if the effort of mind that Lincoln put into his profession had not come out again in his prose. After all, he made his name and rose to the presidency over a question of constitutional law. Legal thought encourages precision through the imagining and the denial of alternatives. The language of the law foresees doubt, ambiguity, confusion, stupid or fraudulent error, and one by one it excludes them. Most lawyers succeed at least in avoiding misunderstanding, and this obviously is the foundation of any prose that aims at clear expression.

As a lawyer Lincoln knew that the courtroom vocabulary would achieve this purpose if handled with a little care. But it would remain jargon, obscure to the common understanding. As an artist, therefore, he undertook to frame his ideas invariably in one idiom, that of daily life. He had to use, of course, the technical names of the actions and documents he dealt with. But all the rest was in the vernacular. His first achievement, then, was to translate the minute accuracy of the advocate and the judge into the words of common men.

To say this is to suggest a measure of Lincoln's struggle as an artist. He started with very little confidence in his stock of knowledge, and having to face audiences far more demanding than ours, he toiled to improve his vocabulary, grammar, and logic. In the first year of his term in Congress he labored through six books of Euclid in hopes of developing the coherence of thought he felt he needed in order to demonstrate his views. Demonstration was to him the one proper goal of argument; he never seems to have considered it within his power to convince by disturbing the judgment through the emotions. In the few passages where he resorts to platform tricks, he uses only irony or satire, never the rain-barrel booming of the Fourth-of-July orator.

One superior gift he possessed from the start and developed to a supreme degree, the gift of rhythm. Take this fragment, not from a finished speech, but from a jotting for a lecture on the law:

"There is a vague popular belief that lawyers are necessarily dishonest. I say vague, because when we consider to what extent confidence and honors are reposed in and conferred upon lawyers by the people, it appears improbable that their impression of dishonesty is very distinct and vivid. Yet the impression is common, almost universal. Let no young man choosing the law for a calling for a moment yield to the popular belief—resolve to be honest at all events; and if in your own judgment you cannot be an honest lawyer, resolve to be honest without being a lawyer."

Observe the ease with which the theme is announced: "There is a vague popular belief that lawyers are necessarily dishonest." It is short without crackling like an epigram, the word "necessarily" retarding the rhythm just enough. The thought is picked up with hardly a pause: "I say vague, because, when we consider . . ." and so on through the unfolding of reasons, which winds up in a kind of calm: "it appears improbable that their impression of dishonesty is very distinct and vivid." Now a change of pace to refresh interest: "Yet the impression is common, almost universal." And a second change, almost immediately, to usher in the second long sentence, which carries the conclusion: "Let no young man choosing the law . . ."

The paragraph moves without a false step, neither hurried nor drowsy; and by its movement, like one who leads another in the dance, it catches up our thought and swings it into willing compliance. The ear notes at the same time that none of the sounds grate or clash: the piece is sayable like a speech in a great play; the music is manly, the alliterations are few and natural. Indeed, the paragraph seems to have come into being spontaneously as the readiest incarnation of Lincoln's thoughts.

From hints here and there, one gathers that Lincoln wrote slowly—meaning, by writing, the physical act of forming letters on paper. This would augment the desirability of being brief. Lincoln wrote before the typewriter and the dictating machine, and wanting to put all his meaning into one or two lucid sentences, he thought before he wrote. The great compression came after he had, lawyerlike, excluded alternatives and hit upon right order and emphasis.

Obviously this style would make use of skips and connections unsuited to speechmaking. The member of the cabinet who received a terse memorandum had it before him to make out at leisure. But an audience requires a looser texture, just as it requires a more measured delivery. This difference between the written and the spoken word lends color to the cliché that if Lincoln had a style, he developed it in his presidential years. Actually, Lincoln, like an artist, adapted his means to the occasion. There was no pathos in him before pathos was due. When he supposed his audience intellectually alert—as was the famous gathering at Cooper Union in 1860—he gave them his concentrated prose. We may take as a sample a part of the passage where he addresses the South:

"Again, you say we have made the slavery question more prominent than it formerly was. We deny it. We admit that it is more prominent, but we deny that we made it so. It was not we, but you, who discarded the old policy of the fathers. We resisted, and still resist, your innovation; and thence comes the greater prominence of the question. Would you have that question reduced to its former proportions? Go back to that old policy. What has been, will be again, under the same conditions. If you would have the peace of the old times, readopt the precepts and policy of the old times."

This is wonderfully clear and precise and demonstrative, but two hours of equally succinct argument would tax any but the most athletic audience. Lincoln gambled on the New Yorkers' agility of mind, and won. But we should not be surprised that in the debates with Stephen A. Douglas, a year and a half before, we find the manner different. Those wrangles lasted three hours, and the necessity for each speaker to interweave prepared statements of policy with improvised rebuttals of charges and "points" gives these productions a coarser grain. Yet on Lincoln's side, the same artist mind is plainly at work:

"Senator Douglas is of world-wide renown. All the anxious politicians of his party, or who have been of his party for years past, have been looking upon him as certainly, at no distant day, to be the President of the United States. They have seen in his round, jolly, fruitful face, post offices, land offices, marshalships, and cabinet appointments, chargéships and foreign missions, bursting and sprouting out in wonderful exuberance ready to be laid hold of by their greedy hands."

The man who could lay the ground for a splendid yet catchy metaphor about political plums by describing Douglas's face as round, jolly and *fruitful* is not a man to be thought merely lucky in the handling of words. The debates abound in happy turns, but read less well than Lincoln's more compact productions. Often, Douglas's words are more polished:

"We have existed and prospered from that day to this thus divided and have increased with a rapidity never before equaled in wealth, the extension of territory, and all the elements of power and greatness, until we have become the first nation on the face of the globe. Why can we not thus continue to prosper?"

It is a mistake to underrate Douglas's skill, which was that of a professional. Lincoln's genius needs no heightening through lowering others. Douglas was smooth and adroit, and his arguments were effective, since Lincoln was defeated. But Douglas—not so Lincoln—sounds like anybody else.

Lincoln's extraordinary power was to make his spirit felt, a power I attribute to his peculiar relation to himself. He regarded his face and physique with amusement and dismay, his mind and destiny with wonder. Seeming clumsy and diffident, he also showed a calm superiority which he expressed as if one half of a double man were talking about the other.

In conduct, this detachment was the source of his saintlike forebearance; in his art, it yielded the rare quality of elegance. Nowhere is this link between style and emotional distance clearer than in the farewell Lincoln spoke to his friends in Springfield before leaving for Washington. A single magical word, easy to pass over carelessly, holds the clue:

"My friends: No one, not in my situation, can appreciate my feeling of sadness at this parting. To this place, and the kindness of these people, I owe everything. . . ." If we stop to think, we ask: "This place"?—yes. But why "*these* people"? Why not "you people," whom he was addressing from the train platform, or "this place and the kindness of *its* people"? It is not, certainly, the mere parallel of *this* and *these* that commanded the choice. "These" is a stroke of genius, which betrays Lincoln's isolation from the action itself—Lincoln talking to himself about the place and the people whom he was leaving, foreboding the possibility of his never returning, and closing the fifteen lines with one of the greatest cadences in English speech: "To His care commending you, as I hope in your prayers you will commend me, I bid you an affectionate farewell."

The four main qualities of Lincoln's literary art—precision, vernacular ease, rhythmical virtuosity, and elegance—may at a century's remove seem alien to our tastes. Yet it seems no less odd to question their use and interest to the present when one considers one continuing strain in our literature. Lincoln's example, plainly, helped to break the monopoly of the dealers in literary plush. After Lincoln comes Mark Twain, and out of Mark Twain come contemporaries of ours as diverse as Sherwood Anderson, H. L. Mencken, and Ernest Hemingway. Lincoln's use of his style for the intimate genre and for the sublime was his alone; but his workaday style is the American style par excellence.

[1959]

6   Poe As Proofreader

Among the attributes with which Poe endowed the detective story, an indispensable one, and perhaps the most congenial to him, was pedantry. Obviously, the detective must see farther into a brick wall than other men, and he must know what he knows with a niggling precision—think of the significance in "The Gold Bug" of seeing the rough sketch on dirty parchment as a kid instead of a goat. With success rewarding his hairsplitting, the detective becomes an inveterate show-off and pedant.

To say this is to say that the spirit of science and scholarship informs the detective story, a truth which justifies the critics when they in turn pounce on flaws in detective fiction which in other works it would be unworthy to notice.

Now in Poe's favorite among his four tales of ratiocination, "The Purloined Letter," there is a paragraph which has always troubled me pedantically—about its author and about his editors. It is the one, a few pages from the end of the story, which compares the bright schoolboy's skill in outguessing his fellows with the psychologizing that has given a reputation of "spurious profundity to Rochefoucault, La Bougive, Machiavelli, and Campanella."

Let us begin ratiocinating about the first two names. Poe professed to know a good deal about French and its literature. He ends this very tale with a couplet from an obscure tragedy by Crébillon (*Atrée et Thyeste,* 1707); and as everybody knows, three out of his four detective stories are set in Paris and present a French nobleman as hero. Yet in the passage I refer to, Poe writes Rochefoucault with a barely allowable *t* instead of *d,* and without the obligatory *La* before the name. Next and worse, he cites a certain *La Bougive,* who by a majority vote of Poe's editors has been accepted as real.

I mean by majority vote that since Poe's day only a handful of editors, reprinters, or introducers of the tale have changed the supposititious name to the one obviously meant: La Bruyère. In 1845 Evert Duyckinck brought out a volume of Poe's *Tales,* a copy of which, known as the Lorimer Graham copy, was annotated by Poe himself in 1849. Among Poe's marks scattered through the pages there is no correction of either Rochefoucault or La Bougive.

But why should an author be a good proofreader of his works? The chances are rather the other way; he pursues sense and supplies it mentally in defiance of print. It is his editors who should repair his oversights. I have looked up "The Purloined Letter" in forty-one editions and reprints, beginning with the notorious and confusing issue of the *Works* in 1850, immediately after Poe's death. I have looked into single volumes and large sets, anthologies and fancy illustrated gift books, and nearly everywhere I have found La Bougive surviving.

The great University of Virginia edition of 1902 in seventeen volumes, reissued in 1965, corrects Rochefoucault to *d* (without *La*) and makes a point of it in the notes, but it embalms La Bougive. The Quinn edition with a specially "established" text (Knopf, 1958) has the old *t* and the old fraud. It repeats, in short, these errors of the 1850 *Works* which presumably had passed through the hands of N. P. Willis, R. W. Griswold, James Russell Lowell, and others.

In the 1870s and 1880s Richard Henry Stoddard left the text untouched for his often reprinted six-volume edition, and so it has continued down to our times. Persons of learning and judgment such as Hervey Allen, Padraic Colum, Killis Campbell, Clifton Fadiman, W. H. Auden, E. H. Davidson, Addison Hibbard, Philip Van Doren Stern, Laurence Meynell, Lee Wright, and Ellery Queen, among others, seem to authenticate the nonsense. Of course, they probably never saw the text being reprinted, or they read it with Poe's unseeing eye —though the late Hervey Allen in his Modern Library introduction rather prides himself on scholarship and textual accuracy.

The first corrected English text (for Baudelaire as translator had naturally used the genuine name) seems to be the *Tales and Poems* edited by John H. Ingram and issued by John C. Nimmo in London in 1884 (at the same time as the tales only, by Tauchnitz on the Continent). Ten years elapsed before an American editor followed suit, namely Poe's biographer, George Edward Woodberry, who brought out with Edmund Clarence Stedman a ten-volume edition of the works (Chicago, 1894). The English have been more often right (e.g., Dorothy Sayers in her *Tales of Detection,* Everyman, 1936); the Americans are conservative. How do we stand now?

In 1968 there were eighteen editions of Poe's tales in print in this country, all but two of them containing "The Purloined Letter." Among these reprints are the justly respected Modern Library, Riverside, Holt, Viking, Blue Ribbon, Everyman, and World's Classics series. All but the last-named prolong the existence of La

Bougive. On La Rochefoucauld there is much variation, which suggests that some editors or writers of introductions have read proof and taken a little thought—yet not enough.

Having sunk so far in pedantry, I was interested to see what readers in three presumable centers of culture—New York, Boston-Cambridge, and Princeton-Lawrenceville—had available on this great matter in the public and semipublic libraries of the vicinage. With the aid of friends I gathered data which show that the texts within reach overwhelmingly persuade the young, the innocent, the gullible, *and the blind* of the reality of La Bougive. It is time that some conscientious editor-scholar should compose posthumous works by La Bougive answering to Poe's curious intention in citing him.

For there are one or two questions more baffling than nomenclature arising out of the troublesome paragraph. First, what exactly is the comparison that Poe has in view? The schoolboy in the tale guesses his opponents' purposes through fashioning his facial expression to match theirs. But he must also "admeasure" his interlocutor's degree of intellect. The reason for this second step is not clear, but never mind. The main device suggests rather the subsequent James-Lange theory of the emotions (=feelings arise from bodily changes) rather than the maxims of the French and Italian moralists. Is Poe saying that these thinkers judged mankind by scanning their own minds? Well, how else is it done?

Moreover, if the schoolboy is deemed acute and successful, why are the comparable results of the four great writers dismissed as "spurious profundity"? Are we to infer that they drew their wisdom by the too simple trick of molding their features into the likeness of those they spoke to—from Cesare Borgia to the courtiers at Versailles? Probably all that Poe meant was that maxims about mankind are at once too easy to write and too unreliable. If so, he wrapped up that commonplace in the spurious profundity of the great detective when talking to his Watson and his public.

Remains the question of Poe's knowledge of French. In two of his letters he advises a friend to bother as little as possible with grammar and "to read *side-by-side* translations continually, of which there are many to be found." Did Poe use the same uncertain method? He quotes Crébillon and others, I must say, without error. But his casual words and phrases show the usual English speaker's confusions. I do not merely mean faults of inattention such as *intriguant* for *intrigant*; I mean the clear evidence that Poe lacked the feel of the language. He may have been to Russia: he certainly never visited Paris. Else in the title of "The Murders in the Rue Morgue" he would not have gained compression at the expense of idiom: the only possible phrase is *rue de la Morgue*.[1]

Again, Poe asks us to believe that his hero, descended from an illustrious family, lived like an aesthete in rooms situated *au troisième, No. 33 rue Dunôt*. These accents are illicit, like those in the names of Marie Rogêt, *rue des Drômes*, and Isidore Musèt.[2] Poe apparently imagined that the accent makes the linguist; the French have had their revenge by dressing him up as Edgar Poë.

Still, a light-handed blue pencil could set all this right.

1. In Poe's day the Paris morgue was not on a *rue* at all, but on the quai du Marché Neuf, beyond the Petit Pont.

2. That is, if *dromes* is the common noun. If a proper noun, then the plural makes nonsense. See also the atrocities of accent, gender, and number in his humorous story *Bon-Bon*.

What cannot be altered is the implausibility of more functional parts, e.g., "C. Auguste Dupin." The form initial-plus-given-name is unknown in French. It is primarily English and occasionally (anglophile) American. As for chevaliers, they went out with the old régime; and even positing the idea of a proud émigré, the inventor of his name should have produced something with a *de* after *chevalier* and something else before du Pin, in two words. As it stands, Auguste Dupin spells the commoner, not the chevalier. It is the same sort of connotative error, fatal to a detective, that makes the words *Mon dieu!* in the Rue Morgue story inadequate to playing their part in the ratiocination.

There it is: Poe's French was from Stratford atte Bowe; the scraps of it scattered throughout his works show that when not quoting from an open book Poe stumbles. Nor does it matter at all, of course, except in detective fiction. There, as I hope to have shown, fallibility is a crime. La Bougive (and Campanella, whom I have not read but suspect of irrelevance) spoil the broth, and the other trifles make us groan. The least that Poe's American admirers could have done, long since, was to give La Bougive a soft quietus and restore what Poe had undoubtedly written in his precise round hand.[3] Imagine having to wait a century and a quarter for an editor to tamper with your text!

[1970]

3. See "The Man in the Crowd" for a quotation from La Bruyère with his name correctly spelled.

7 The Bibliographer and His Absence of Mind

One of the advantages of living in the twentieth century is that there is no longer need to worry about the *cogito ergo sum*. Today, a reference book supplies the desired proof of actuality, gives the best warrant of true existence. If something sought or something thought turns up in some Index or other, then it *is*. Look it up and it's real; look me up, *ergo sum*. I tested this by leafing through the *Yellow Pages for Manhattan* (1968), and was rewarded with the evidence that even philosophers are solid entities: that unimpeachable book of reference certifies the existence of two metaphysicians—no doubt one Platonist and one Aristowhatsit.

Extending the test, those of us who have long enjoyed mystery stories *sub judice* can now dwell secure in the knowledge that the genre is, in metaphysical parlance, a *tertium quid*. It has found its referencer who points with his thick Index and says in effect, "Thar she blows!" Thanks to his marching columns of print, the literature is no longer fugitive; it occupies permanent shelf space, its survival is more certain than that of ripe fruit or the difference between the sexes.

The new Index numbers 834 large pages—half a million words—a tome that the future archaeologist will dig up and use to demonstrate the general proposition that by one avenue of interest or another, we in this century were fundamentally tomists. My play on words is inspired by the apt one in the title of the book before me.[1] The publishers are to be congratulated for their courage in making it and thereby recognizing the progeny of Poe's great creation of 125 years ago.

It may surprise that I congratulate the publishers rather than the author. One good reason is that it is their material product, four pounds net of paper and cloth, that confers the reality I celebrate. There is a second reason, equally good, which later comments will disclose. Here I want to describe what the new volume brings. It opens with 420 pages of double-column alphabetical listing by authors. Under each name are the titles of the writer's works, with publishers' names and dates of publication. According to the compiler, the "books have been classified as (D) Detective, (M) Mystery, and (S) Suspense. . . ." But this is inexact. The *authors* have been so classified and designated, with a resulting inaccuracy about *books* that is to be deplored.

Following the main section is a series of shorter ones, under the misleading caption "Bibliographic Guide." One section purports to group some of the tales by subject and setting; another lists the films and plays based on, or created as, stories of the kind; still another gives a roster of heroes, *et cetera*. Finally, we reach more genuine bibliography in the listing of anthologies, collections, and critical writings on the genre. After this comes a miscellany—quotations, anecdotes, biographical paragraphs—and at the end an index of titles. In this last

1. Ordean A. Hagen, *Who Done It? An Encyclopedic Guide to Detective, Mystery, and Suspense Fiction* (New York: R. R. Bowker, 1969).

feature lies the chief merit of the work: errors excepted, it links some twenty-five thousand titles with their authors.

While the work was in preparation, a note about it in a literary weekly stated that the compiler had begun reading for it two years before. That was the fatal step. The assumption was that one could make a reference book out of other reference books—the catalogs of the Library of Congress and the British Museum, the Penguin and other publishers' lists, the catalogs of specialized second-hand dealers, and various writings on the genre that included bibliographies.

Trusting these, the well-meaning adventurer fell dupe to the metaphysical fantasy with which I opened this review. The many, many errors of fact and blunders of judgment in these 800 pages come from taking as real what is said in some other books, mistaking information on index cards for knowledge of the literature. Anyone can see why this procedure breeds howlers in rabbitlike profusion—the card leaves no trace in the mind, no distinct idea, no sense of the plausible, no familiar substance by which errors already in print can be rectified and new ones avoided.

For example, in his grouping of a few tales by scenes and subjects—in itself a good intention—the compiler has the category Hospitals. Under it we read: "Rhode, John, the Dr. Priestley novels." Now anyone who has ever read a Rhode story knows that Dr. Priestley is a mathematician and physicist, not a "doctor." The serious student knows further that of the more than one hundred Rhode novels, not one is laid in a hospital, although at least three concern physicians. Compounding his error, our classifier omits Josephine Bell, a physician-author who has used the hospital scene in several stories, and has a novel explicitly called *Murder in Hospital*. Last and worst, there is no mention of the masterpiece that comes first to mind. *The Nursing-Home Murder,* by Ngaio Marsh and Dr. Jellett. But then one must have read the book to know that "Nursing-Home" is not what the title may suggest: the story takes place in and around an operating room.

Such essential details cannot be summoned up out of catalogs, and they do not figure reliably in this one. Nor is the consequence peculiar to our subject or any other. Any violation of the simple rules of scholarship has fated results of the kind that make one ask about the present work: "Will it help anyone at all?" One wonders for whom it was compiled: Will it not confuse the seeker and dishearten the browser?

Consider the last first. Some readers are attracted more by the scene of a story than by its kind: they will read anything about an academic institution or a fashion designer's shop. If such a reader turns to the group Universities and Colleges, he will find two titles that denote but one story, another that doesn't belong there—and (if one may be said to find what is missing) several classics overlooked. Again, there is no class Fashion, although there should be, if only to transfer a title mistakenly put under Advertising. Likewise, Schools (a larger and better group than Colleges) has entirely escaped the compiler's notice. Note that these deficiencies are culled from one small section of the work, which is built throughout on the same shaky foundation.

It is discouraging. I find no pleasure in detailing the inadequacy of what must have cost many months of drudgery. I know how bewildering and baffling the state of the literature is. What with the paperback stampede and the different notions of England and America about what sounds enticing, many stories have appeared under two or more titles; identical titles (or nearly) belong to different stories; and the proliferation of pseudonyms is numbing to the mind. But these are the very reasons why a bibliography is needed and why it should never have come from an innocent card shuffler. It was proper work for a rum-soaked reader of detective fiction, preferably 120 years old.

A reader so qualified would long since have met and solved the worst bibliographic puzzle by sheer longevity. Difficulties iron themselves out if one waits attentive in the right spot. A typical confusion from *Who Done It?* will make this clear. The works of Father Ronald Knox are not easy to find, and their frequent double titling is a cause of perplexity. What our "guide" says about a pair of his works is unfortunately not true. Knox's *Double Cross Purposes* is not the same as *Settled Out of Court* (which is also *The Body in the Silo*).

Such an error may seem trivial relatively to a large number of titles, but bibliography should, after all, tell us what is what without differentiating between large and small facts. A title is a clue for hunting down a book. Well, without purposely looking for duplicates—how *could* one?—my eye quickly spotted fourteen stories that are made to look like twenty-eight by being listed again under different titles. Think of the time wasted looking for one more (nonexistent) tale by a favorite author!

Our bibliographer, moreover, gives no indication when a title covers a collection of short stories; nor does he care whether he leads you into subjects not germane to his announced concern. He has listed far too many novels that have nothing to do with detection, mystery, or suspense. There are at least five under Joanna Cannan, five under Jacques Futrelle, six under Georgette Heyer, three under Eden Phillpotts, and singletons under a multitude of other authors. Nonfiction is also intermixed, for example: *She Stands Accused* (MacClure) is a series of biographical sketches of women criminals; *The Green Bicycle Case* (Wakefield) is the analysis of a famous English homicide of 1919; *Crime in Our Time* (Bell) is a sociological study; *Fingerprints* (Browne and Brock) should have given itself away as a treatise.

Some other books are well-known novels of other kinds. *The Four Feathers* (Mason) is a story of courage and fidelity; *Cypress Man* (Lewis) is a novel of artistic egotism; *The Sorrows of Satan* (Corelli) is a one-time best seller about religion. As for the popular *Wallet of Kai Lung* (Bramah) it is, as everybody knows, a collection of humorous anecdotes in pseudo-Chinese, and the wallet is not, as the bibliographer apparently imagined, a temptation for the thief. Nor is *The Thief* (Croft-Cooke)— any more than two others under his name—a detective story, but a study of character and circumstance.

At this point the purchaser even more than the reviewer will ask: Who guides the guide when he's lost? The frustrated user will easily gauge the extent of his own bediddlement. Amid the promised (D) (M) (S), he will find technical criminology (Cherrill), sea stories (Hammond Innes), ghost stories, famous trials, adventure stories *(Beau Geste)*, stories of ethical struggle (Balchin, Cozzens), as well as the bare listing of the complete works of O. Henry, Ambrose Bierce, Henry James and Jorge Luis Borges. Is this bibliography? But editorial insouciance does not stop there. Since, as is well known, everything in French literature is mysterious, we are given titles at random from the translated works of Michel Butor, Marcel Aymé, and Alain Robbe-Grillet; and for good measure, the somber sexual-religious tale by Georges Bernanos called in English *Crime*.

It was of course a conceivable plan to bring together with mystery and detection certain neighboring genres: true crime, famous trials, the practice and theory of detection criminal psychology, historical mysteries, and ghost stories. The juxtaposition would have served a wide yet unified public, *provided* the books were clearly designated for what they were, lest the vacationing philosopher in his hammock break his teeth over criminal psychiatry when he was only eager for crime.

In the present book not only is no clear distinction of this sort made, but none is made between the dissimilar works of a versatile writer. And worse, the jumble of various kinds of authors that we have just sampled is not consistently carried out. If Kipling's *Phantoms and Fantasies* shows the wish to represent the ghost story, why no entry for M. R. James, one of its greatest masters? If H. G. Wells supplies the taste for science fiction, why is Conan Doyle's suppressed and Jules Verne's unlisted, to say nothing of their numerous followers? Why the fiction of Chekhov and nothing by Dostoevski? Why the skimpy choice from Bulwer Lytton and nothing from Balzac, who is full of crime? Dickens is there with *Edwin Drood,* but why *Bleak House* beside it and not *Our Mutual Friend*—or the short pieces about ghosts and policemen? Arnold Bennett shows up with his war horse, but one wonders why Muriel Spark appears at all.

Again, if a marginal relevance suffices, why not Trollope's *Eustace Diamonds,* Julian Hawthorne's series about Inspector Byrnes, and the interesting ventures in mystery of Lord Dunsany and Donn Byrne, Brander Matthews and A. P. Herbert? The so-called selection made here is worse than capricious—it is downright careless, as when we are invited to read Henry James's *Two Magics* only to find the second tale in it to be a love story. We might have preferred the ghastly crime in *The Other House,* which is not listed.

The probable answer to all these queries is that our bibliographer is not at home in general literature either. But then why not stick to his last and make a systematic effort to take down from the shelf the books in the three genres defined by his subtitle? It is understandable that he could not read twenty thousand run-of-the-mill stories, many of which have perished; but there were five thousand about which genuine information would have been worth having. It is no excuse to say as he does in his Preface: "There may even be books in this bibliography which are not mystery, detective, or suspense titles." Quite so. Only a miracle, no doubt, kept out *Moby Dick,* with Melville labeled (S).

If correct information about books (and their titles) is too much to expect, what about the real dope on authors? Librarian-fashion, authors are listed in these pages under their real names, which is not a serviceable scheme for *readers,* it being normal to associate one's literary pleasures with the writer's literary name. George Eliot is a great novelist; Mary Ann Evans is only the pedant's girl friend. Similarly, it is John Rhode (not Major Street) who is so indefatigable and Joanna Cannan who is so charming—not Mrs. H. J. Pullein-Thompson. Moreover, in several important cases of double or triple pseudonyms that go with different types of story, the reader is greatly inconvenienced by their merger under one name. He may, for example, prefer Barnaby Ross to Ellery Queen and have to comb through three and a half columns headed Dannay to find the five books he wants.

Besides, the questionable system is not consistently carried out. Anthony Boucher's works are listed under that pen name, although the author was William Anthony Parker White. More mysterious still, Neville Brand heads the book entry when just above is the rubric: Charles Neville Brand. Gelett Burgess is misrepresented as a pseudonym for one "Justin Sturgis." A Julian Sturgis did exist, the author of two books not related to any of the subjects in hand. The depth of absurdity is reached when we are told that Hilaire Belloc is a pseudonym, the "real name" being Joseph Hilaire Pierre Belloc.

As for the chaotic handling of the women writers' first names, married names, and pseudonyms, it defies description. No married name is given for Dorothy Sayers, although Margery Allingham's is acknowledged; Ngaio Marsh's first name (Edith) is not given, although others are; and when we track down "Joseph Shearing" and his copseudonyms, we get the following: Shearing refers us to "Long, Mrs. Gabrielle"; Marjorie Bowen to "Long, Gabrielle Margaret"; George Preedy to "Long, Mrs. Gabrielle Margaret";—we're creeping up on it!—finally, under Long, we find: "Mrs. Gabrielle Margaret Vere Campbell." I do not care one way or the other about these nameful orgies, but if our attention is drawn to them, the bibliographer owes us the courtesy of order and system.

His failure here is the proof for all time that the pure-card method, unencumbered by any knowledge of books, is meant by the gods to land one in the gravest kind of folly: Matthew Head is the pseudonym of the art critic John Canaday. One of his excellent detective stories, based on wartime work in Africa, is called *Congo Venus*. By the librarian's rule this book is listed with others under Canaday. But the roving eye starts from its socket on finding that same title under "Allison Barbara Neville," an English writer of crime stories involving doctors. It is unlikely that *Congo Venus* would be appropriate for any work of hers. What is the explanation? It is that the Englishwoman's pseudonym is Edward Candy —Canaday-Candy: the mixing of slips is the making of slips.[2]

Dare I go on, still with the potential browser in mind? Heartfree and hopeful, what are his needs? Clear directions. A bibliographer knows that omnibus volumes and collections of short stories overlap endlessly in contents and titles—but not this bibliographer. The result is that half of the twenty titles under Raymond Chandler are of no use as they stand. They have been dumped there,

2. I cannot tell how many similar confusions bespangle the pages of *Who Done It?*, but in my one run-through I have found two besides the one above: (1) Doris Ball = Josephine Bell, and Harold Blundell = George Bellairs. Result: Bell's *Death at Half Term* appears again under Blundell. (2) Because there is a Janet Caird and a Catherine Aird, K. H. McIntosh (who is Miss Aird) is made into a Catherine Caird and credited with one of the two Aird stories.

not *entered*. Just as it helps to know the English and American titles for any one story, so it would help to be told that Chandler's *Simple Art of Murder* covers two unlike groupings of tales and other prose, and that some of the short stories recur in collections with unlike titles. If bibliography is not to disentangle just these snarls, it is nothing.

Beyond that elementary service the reader is entitled to reasonable completeness. Yet on every page of this inventory the connoisseur will find omissions. Obvious gaps occur in such entries as: Anthony Armstrong, Leslie Beresford, George Birmingham, Joseph L. Bonney, Eric Bruton, G. V. Galwey, John Godwin, M. R. Hodgkin, Mark Twain, A. A. Milne, William Mole, Simon Nash, Oliver Onions, Jeremy Potter, David Sharp, and a dozen more.

If one wanted to be really demanding, one would also look for the forerunners of the detective genre, none of whom appears in the guide: Voltaire, Beaumarchais, James Fenimore Cooper, Alexander Dumas, William Leggett. The treatment of Poe himself is bibliographically speaking a crime. Here is the founder of the genre, and the three references given consist of a paperback (hence hard of access), a selection not in print, and the Everyman edition of the *Tales*. The date given for this last volume (1908/1931) would suggest that it too is out of print, whereas the latest reissue is 1966. Meanwhile there are on the market a dozen excellent reprints of the stories; and on the library shelves some twenty-five older editions.

In a large work of this kind—especially in its first printing—it is inevitable that many typographical errors

should have escaped the author in proofreading, and
even earlier, in typescript. But a proper question about
typos is—how many and of what kind? In *Who Done It?*
the number is excessive and some of the kinds unforgiv-
able. It is merely irritating that the putting or omitting
of *A* and *The* before titles should be fitful, but when the
articles are interchanged, the result can be infuriating,
for example, J. C. Masterman's *An Oxford Tragedy* is
made inept by being recast as *The Oxford Tragedy*.
Other errors are as bad: Bruce Hamilton's *Too Much of
Water,* which is a quotation from Shakespeare, becomes
silly as *Too Much Water.* Likewise, one resents seeing
Bellairs's *Case of the Seven Whistlers* changed to *Whis-
tles;* Crofts's *Futile Alibi* turned into *Future Alibi;*
Bowers's *Deed without a Name* with *Deed* changed to
Dead; and Crispin's *Dead and Dumb* caricatured as
Death and Dumb. And readers will stare when they get
hold of the books after tracking down Brock's *Dagwort
Coombie Mystery* (for *Combe*) and Crofts's *Mr. Hefton
Murders,* whose title is: *Mr. Sefton, Murderer.*

Indeed the letter *s* flits without warrant from one title
to another, but literal malpractice does not become really
offensive until it attacks proper names. It is bad to have
John Beynon misspelled Benyon, because it changes the
alphabetical order; normal care would have ensured the
right spelling of Victor MacClure and the correct se-
quence and spelling of Barbara Alison Neville; it is
worse to have Marion Rous Hodgkin (wife of Alan
Hodgkin, the famous scientist) turned into Hodgin, and
it is outrageous to find Bennett Copplestone (with an
extra *t* in Bennet) preceded by an imaginary Bennett
Cobblestone six pages earlier. The same slovenliness
creates a place for one Dermet Marrah (falsely tagged *M*

as a writer) fifteen pages before the actual Dermot Macgregor Morrah, rightly tagged *D,* but deprived of the Michael to which he is entitled.

The handling of names and ranks is in fact culpably erratic throughout. The bibliographer, as we know, professes to give the multiple names of married women, but suddenly G. D. H. Cole's wife and collaborator is "M. I.," with no indication that M. I. is a woman.[3] Elsewhere titles are set down or omitted capriciously—C. P. Snow and John Cecil Masterman without Lord or Sir, but "Baron John Buchan Tweedsmuir" (properly, "J. B., baron T."). Other barons—Gorell, Charnwood, Clanmorris—receive their full spread, but with no knowledge of the system, and with a good chance that we shall go and ask for the works of "Lord Barnes." Again, a pair of entries gives Hamilton, E. W., and Hamilton, Lord Frederic Spencer, although both were lords, the sixth and fourth sons respectively of the Duke of Abercorn, Lord Ernest being the author of that little masterpiece: *The Four Tragedies of Memworth.*

Finally, we stumble across the odd entry: Collaboration. Under it two titles are listed which show that the heading means: "Various Hands"—one tale by half a dozen writers. The best examples (*Ask a Policeman* and *Floating Admiral*) are not among those listed, of which one is very likely misplaced. *Ask a Policeman* our bibliographer erroneously puts much farther on, under Anthologies, and in his description forgets three of the famous collaborators, including the architect of this well-knit work, John Rhode.

Time after time, then, the guide fails to guide. One finds

3. Nor are we told that *The Brooklyn Murders* was written by G. D. H. alone, the first of the fifty.

holes in the listing of plays, of film actors, of theorists about the detective genre. The delightful *Handbook* by members of Mystery Writers of America and edited by Herbert Brean is missing; and so is the collection of essays gathered by Michael Gilbert; the work by Martienssen on the British police is mislabeled a critique of fictional crime, and there is no reference to any of the detailed studies of our glorious tradition by such foreign writers as Caillois, Wölcken, Michaud, Narcejac, and others.[4] Lastly, in his skimpy glossary of terms of art the bibliographer does not give the origin of the warning letters HIBK; and he is wrong on the current English use of "thriller," as well as on the source and primary meaning of "gunsel."

In the two hundred pages of back matter exclusive of the index, the compiler has ventured on opinions. With the best will in the world one cannot say that these redeem the rest. The theorist is jocose and deals in commonplaces, one of which affords perhaps the *locus classicus* of tautology:"Detective story—one in which a detective or detectives solve the crime." Elsewhere, the light touch which is obviously intended is only dull colloquialism (". . . they bore the daylights out of you"). This was to be expected, for the light touch can only come from intelligent familiarity, and the entire compendium, as I have been forced to show, has been done on the opposite principle, the principle of remote control.

The moral—and it is no trifling one—is that in works of the mind remoteness nullifies control. This would-be bibliography is a product of uncontrolled promiscuity among twenty-five thousand cards. Both the text and the

4. To make up for this, perhaps, an essay of mine appears twice.

compiler's acknowledgments to his family and friends suggest that the work was put together from notes absentmindedly taken, then transcribed by amanuenses who were willing but uncomprehending slaves (see Cobblestone).

True, for the last thirty years the academic world has done everything to make possible this apotheosis. Although achieved single-handed, it gives us a foretaste of the scholarship of the future, when ingenious but ignorant computer programmers will cast their secondhand data in a metalanguage designed to yield new knowledge without leg- or brainwork—the armchair detective indeed, asleep in his chair. Fortunately for the comfort of those future scholars and their readers, everybody by then will be as happy as if the results squared with direct experience. For that experience will be deemed primitive, superseded, irrelevant, the consumers of books having long since forgotten that knowledge grows only out of knowledge and not out of information.

[1969]

8 Behind the Blue Pencil: Censorship or Creeping Creativity?

One of the main differences between British and American publishing lies in the role assigned to the copy editor. Books from London often show inconsistencies of form—say in footnotes or citations—and other evidences of inattention as well. And British authors who are being published in the United States for the first time freely resent (and ignore) the endless queries, suggestions, and alterations that some unnamed hand has sprinkled over their finished work.

The cause of these phenomena is the license given in this country to the copy editor (now more often called manuscript editor). That some additions to the script on its way to the compositor (now more often "the keyboarder") are needed can be granted at once. The correction of typos, the striking out of hyphens at the end of lines, the indication of em-dashes, together with the assigning of point size to heads and subheads, can no longer be left to the judgment and taste of printers, because of the great variety of designs, the decline of artisanship, and the substitution of the typewriter and its offspring for the author's own hand.

But out of the need for this intervention has grown a practice which latterly has been changing the very idea of authorship. There is nothing new in the fact that it is now impossible to know a writer's usage in punctuation or spelling. What appears in print over his name is the punctuation and spelling of "the house" or the individual editor. But within the last few years the rest of a writer's proper business—diction, grammar, idiom, and syntax—has also fallen under the editor's sway; these matters of style are not the free choice of the ostensible author, but rather of the anonymous co-author brought in after the author has said his last word.

The original intention of such a postmortem review was no doubt worthy; it was to spare the author (and the firm) embarrassment over errors—slips of the pen or of the mind, to which every writer is liable and for whose correction before print he is duly grateful.

But soon other tendencies and purposes began to distort that intention. The spread of specialized knowledge, coupled with that of half-education, created a new class of authors—people who knew things of value but wrote badly. For the sake of their information, the publisher in effect appointed a semi-ghost to assist the inarticulate and illiterate. It continues to be true that a good half of the scripts accepted for publication by book and magazine editors are "first-rate stuff but needs a lot of work"—these words are virtually a technical term of the trade.

At the same time, a misplaced regard for science and technology has made the common mind avid for trivial details and correspondingly fearful of small errors. In reading matter now, so long as the date of birth and the middle initial are correct, one can indulge with impunity in the most whopping errors of sense and judgment. To ensure this perfection in trifles, researchers and copy editors painstakingly scan and scribble, after which the author, faced with his guilt and humbled by the many changes, nods his consent. It is a far cry from the attitude of Sir Isaac Newton, who prevented a misprint from being corrected in his *Principia,* saying that competent readers would automatically correct it for themselves.

Partly because editors know that they are dealing with small things and wish to enlarge their scope, and partly because their task lies within the narrowest range of what may be right or wrong, they have begun to challenge and change in written work whatever deviates from their own norm. This raises a question which is rather important for the art of prose: who is this editor and where has he or she picked up that norm?

In the nature of things, editing copy cannot be one of the high, and highly paid, professions. The great majority of manuscript editors are recent college graduates "interested in publishing." The older, experienced ones tend to be free-lance workers at home—any person with good eyesight and who is conscientious can learn the routine. Only for encyclopedias, technical works, and the like, is knowledge of subject matter required. But all copy editors show a common bias: vigilance breeds suspicion, and the suspect is the writer. What he has set down is ipso facto questionable and incomplete; anything not utterly usual is eccentric and reprehensible; what the editor would prefer is preferable.

Before describing the misconceptions, intellectual and literary, that underlie the present extensive revision of works that do not need it, let me illustrate the practice by examples from recent experience, mine and that of colleagues who have expressed their deep annoyance—sometimes their rage—at having to reread and restore their text in order to make it truly theirs in sense and sound. The reason for exploding in private is that the ritual of altering and reversing alterations has come to be seen by all parties as the price paid for being published.

Original Wording:	Altered to:
consecutiveness	continuity
solely an historian	not a mere historian
founded an empire	created an empire
refused their minds	closed their minds
several instances	various instances
Donald Duck	Mickey Mouse
has got out of hand	has gotten out of hand
the remark fitted the case	the remark fit the case
not so many as	not as many as
But he soon gave up	However, he soon gave up
for they thought	because they thought
in this printing	as of this printing
sent to whoever was in charge	sent to whomever was in charge

In this random sampling one finds not merely the wilful substitution of one idea for another but at least four gross mistakes inserted as improvements. In the first five changes the editor was clearly incapable of distinguishing meanings. Continuity is not the same thing as consecutiveness. Several instances are not necessarily various—and so with the rest.

In the Donald Duck example, the text referred to the fiftieth anniversary of that creation. The editor evidently missed the news report of this historic occasion and preferred to cite—heedlessly—a character she thought even more universal.

The next three "improvements" show a leaning toward colloquial, indeed rural, usage; and in any case all three originals are entirely clear, usual, in no need of amendment. In the two that follow, *but* and *for* are disallowed in favor of longer, more textbookish words that are thought equivalent, though they are not. Comment is superfluous on the *as of* borrowed from business English and the grammatical blunder *to whomever is*.

This last error springs from plain ignorance in the very domain where editing lays down the law. But that deficiency is not limited to matters of language. Few copy editors have had time for wide reading before they start on their peculiar form of censorship. They have been to college, and they are not much further advanced by the books they read in the way they have to read them. As a result, they remain unaware of certain idioms, allusions, and conventions that are by no means abstruse. For example, an author who used in the proper context "the liquid element" found the phrase crossed out, the word *water* substituted, and the marginal comment: "Pompous, don't you think?"

That the term was traditional for one of "the four elements" was something as unsuspected by the corrector as the convention governing the citation of proper names. On this point a colleague relates how a book review she wrote came out editorially peppered with needless first names—*John* Mill (*sic*), *Matthew* Arnold, and so on. When she remonstrated she was told, "But there were two authors with those last names!" That one writes *James* Mill and *Thomas* Arnold when referring to the less famous pair was a new idea. There were also two English poets named Pope and two historians of England named Macaulay, but fortunately editors have never heard of the obscure ones, or we would have to trot out "Alexander" and "Thomas Babington" at every turn.

Proper names are also linked with the editorial assumption that every article or chapter must supply all facts and prove 100 percent educational—an encyclopedia entry. And so first names, dates, titles are added in full, often to the detriment of good writing and sometimes of its accuracy. Thus a contributor to the *New York Times* was recently taken to task for referring to "Chief Justice Oliver Wendell Holmes." He replied: "The error was not mine, but in the final editing, which I did not review before publication; my manuscript referred to the Justice simply as 'Holmes.'" I may add that for years now I have lived in that certainty that when I write *Buffon* I shall find *Georges* stuck in front of it in my edited text. The editor, who possibly has never heard of Buffon, looks him up to find a first name—any first name—so as to make sure that no one will confuse him with another: think of the Bach family! Of course, there was but one great naturalist of the name, and—what is too bad—no such person as Georges Buffon ever existed. Georges Leclerc, Comte de Buffon is what one must write if one is to nurse the copy editor's dream of full disclosure. Meanwhile the ancient question occurs: *Quis custodiet,* etc.—"Who will cuss the custodians?"

So far, I have dealt only with meaning in the sense of denotation; but there is the apt use of connotation which, when coupled with right rhythm, is the prerequisite of all good prose, prose that says what the author thinks *and feels,* besides being pleasant to read. In the phrases quoted above, for example, a reader unconsciously responds to the distinction that an empire is *founded* by force but *created* by fiat—the difference between Genghis Khan and Disraeli. Similarly, if one writes: "At that time the guitar was not thought of as capable of serious music," the alteration to "was thought not capable" distorts the implication. The first wording describes opinion; the altered one (falsely) describes the instrument.

Copy editors are doubtless too intent on the mechanics of script-marking to give due thought to nuance and rhetoric. They are especially weak on the use of *a* and *the,* which they take out or insert capriciously. For example, I write "deserves a more ecumenical attention"; the *a* is stricken out, which changes the comparison from quality to quantity. In a technical discussion, the wording was: "experience, meaning here the actually lived." Omit *the* because it is a bit unusual and the sense disappears.

The same blindness spoils rhetoric, just as the matching deafness ruins rhythm. A fellow writer turned an old French folk tale into a child's book. He wrote: "The Devil made the bridge very strong; an army could pass over it— even riding elephants." The point here is the exaggeration, which naturally, necessarily, comes as an afterthought. His copy editor killed the point (and the charm) by recasting: "An army, even riding elephants, could pass over it."

It is sentence rhythm that often dictates whether or not one cites a proper name in full (Mill, instead of John Stuart Mill); whether one puts an adjective before or after the noun ("all things necessary" instead of "all necessary things"); whether one writes "the nineties" or the "1890s." But the idol of Consistency dominates the copy editor's religion, and stylistic variations for the ear as for the mind are ruthlessly cut down. In a lifetime of publishing I have not found one "improver" who ever considered rhythm. I incline again to the belief that this is not for want of native ability; the cause lies in the job itself, which develops the visual reflex at the expense of—reflection.

Besides, not being professional writers, copy editors are seldom aware that prose, like any other art, calls for frequent compromise among desirable aims—sound and sense, force and fluidity, clearness and precision, emphasis and nuance, wit and truth. This very need for balance rules out consistency in the use of *any* component of writing. Each sentence and paragraph is a special case. Style itself demands the opposite of mechanical regularity, even in punctuation and capitalization, let alone in the placing of *only,* the splitting of infinitives, the choice of *which* and *that,* and other bugbears of the manuscript scanner.

When such a person does have the ambition to write, the situation is very likely worse. For the creative urge, which already makes for gratuitous tampering at ordinary times, now knows no bounds and produces a virtual rewriting. Not long ago, having recommended a young writer's book to a university press, I was asked for a preface as a condition of publication. I complied, though skeptical about the utility of such prefaces. When copy edited, my brief remarks showed thirty-five alterations in four-and-a-half pages. Only about one-third affected punctuation and the use of capitals.

This impressive performance is not always equaled, but its ratio of words passed and words challenged is not uncommon either. A member of the innocent public may ask, "What does it matter if you are shown these changes and allowed to restore your original?" It matters in time and effort. Rehabilitating four-and-a-half pages is a nuisance; doing the same for a book of 400 pages is a grievance. Nor is this all. No matter how often a conscious writer goes over his copy before publication, he always looks for still better ways of expressing his meaning. He pursues that meaning, his thought. Editor's alterations compel him to watch at the same time for garblings of that thought. Some stand out, flagrant and unashamed; others—commas added, capitals struck down, inversions and omissions, tend to be overlooked amid one's self-corrections. All the *a*'s and *the*'s trifled with, the dashes and semicolons interchanged, require analytic thought to be seen as unacceptable. Even worse, a misplaced sense of fair play comes over the writer when he is put on the defensive: from weighing the changes and arguing his case step by step, he or she comes to think: "After all, should I have it my own way all the time? Let's give the laborious mole a chance to score as often as we decently can."

This is absurd, but it suggests to me a possible way to settle the serious issue I have outlined here, serious because present practice involves a great waste in two persons' lives, because it threatens the authenticity of the published word, and because it tends ever toward flattening out, standardizing—through pedantry, the literal mind, the love of the usual, which are forms of vulgarity.

The deadlock between writer and corrector is produced, obviously, by the opposition of two legitimate interests: publishing only material that is in fairly literate form and putting one's name only to the words one has chosen to write. I believe these interests relate to two classes of work. If, as in my mangled preface, some 120 lines of prose truly require correction once every three lines, then I am not fit to introduce a good book, and those who have published my writings for the past sixty years have been criminally at fault. But if those lines are intelligible as they stand and look like the work of a good craftsman (though some bright young person might prefer changes at regular intervals), then let the copy go untouched, except for the mechanical markings needed by the printer.

Contrariwise, if the preface, article, or book frequently offends grammar and usage, spends too many words on each idea, and baffles common understanding, then let it be assigned to an experienced writer-editor who, with the author's preliminary consent, will put it into publishable shape.

This division would not debar the copy editor of the healthy manuscripts that bypass remedial treatment from raising a few questions, *provided:* (a) that they are well-considered and (b) that they are not incorporated in the copy but written on slips ("flags") attached to the margin. As I said at the outset, every writer is liable to lapses; an ambiguity, a false linkage, or a bit of non-sense (Editor: *stet* hyphen) may escape even close revision. Every writer, too, will be grateful to the publisher's reader who catches such an error and saves him the embarrassment of discovering it for the first time in print. But this form of help in demonstrable need differs *toto caelo* from the promiscuous depredation which has been allowed to become part of publishing and to which writers alone among artists have tamely permitted themselves to submit.

[1985]

Writer contra Medium

9   Paradoxes of Publishing

Perhaps a sociological novel about book publishing has been written and, being exact but not believable, has failed to achieve publication. I do not know. The fact remains that the general educated public in this country, including many authors, knows a good deal less about the book trade than about any other. The few histories of old publishing houses have been extremely reticent and devoted mostly to the vagaries and *bon mots* of authors. We have had the letters of Max Perkins, but no woman has had the courage to confess: "I married a publisher."

One suspects that a true, that is full, anatomy of publishing would be one of melancholy too. For even the decorous *What Happens in Book Publishing*[1] leaves one troubled, grieving, and stirred to set things right. After reading it, one feels like an early nineteenth-century liberal contemplating the unreformed House of Commons. The present volume is to be praised for giving just that impression without intending to. Its treatment is thorough, well-ballasted with facts and figures, and candid enough to protect the attentive reader against the illusions inseparable from decency. Some of the chapters that a young writer should read are: "Copy Editing," by

1. Chandler B. Grannis, ed., *What Happens in Book Publishing* (New York: Columbia University Press, 1957). [A second edition, considerably revised, of Chandler Grannis's book was published in 1967.—EDITOR]

William Bridgwater; "The Role of the Sales Department," by Hardwick Moseley; "Book Advertising," by
Franklin Spier; "Book Publicity," by Louise Thomas;
"Sales Promotion," by Fon W. Boardman Jr.; "The Book
Traveler," by Clinton C. Balmer; "Subsidiary Rights
and Permissions," by Joseph Marks; and "Business Man-
agement and Accounting," by George P. Brockway.

These, like the remaining chapters on special kinds of
books or special forms of distribution, are written by
people actively engaged in doing what they describe, and
thus a source of living examples. The young author
should memorize the dialogue between the book traveler
and the typical bookseller, Miss Jones, in which Mr.
Balmer begins by placing ten copies of Evelyn Waugh's
Men at Arms, to the tune of mildly depreciatory remarks,
then gives a pat to Frederic Prokosch, who has "a fine
literary reputation" but lacks "really satisfactory sales"
(two copies for Miss Jones), and works up to the really
satisfactory Bartlett, thirty-five of whose *Familiar Quotations* are swept up on the shelves in a deft turn of
dialectic.

The author who grasps the point of this scene, and
interprets it in the light of other conditions described in
this authoritative book, will never again make the mistake of supposing that publishing revolves around him
and his work. Indeed, the index lists just one friendly but
solitary remark by John Farrar under "Author: importance of." Author, then, will take it as Premise One that
book publishing is "an economic structure generally
conceded to be chaotic . . . a chronically sick industry."
He will remember the demonstration that, in order to
break even on the publication of an average book in an
edition of 7,500, the publisher would have to sell 7,759

copies. Publishers must therefore rely on subsidiary earnings—from book clubs, motion pictures, and cheap reprints—as well as on a backlist of really trustworthy authors—Bartlett, Fanny Farmer, Emily Post, and the like. Even so, publishers' net profits after taxes these days amount to only 2 percent of sales.

Hence the chameleonic philosophy and uncomfortable stance that publishers have to adopt toward their authors. If the word ambivalence did not exist, it would have to be invented for this relationship.

There is, first, the legacy of the great Author & Publisher war. In spite of good will, and frequently of true friendship, Author and Publisher are natural antagonists. Their opposition is worse than the natural one between buyer and seller, because it is complicated by pretensions and temperament on both sides. Authors, as everybody knows, are difficult—they are unreliable, arrogant, and grasping. But publishers are impossible—grasping, arrogant, and unreliable. Many publishing tangles come from the fact that authors and publishers are far too much alike. They are so, not because all publishers are disappointed authors—this is a false cliché—but simply because their work is indeterminate, fugitive, tantalizing; and this makes them disappointed men, like authors.

And now that most authors have grown used to earning a living apart from authorship, a further split is occurring: authors are becoming more independent and are developing businesslike habits. A writer of average orderliness who is about to be published should brace himself for a strenuous task: keeping the various departments of the firm in touch with one another; seeing to it that what has been decided about design, jacket copy, publicity, and the like is done, and not some other thing talked of earlier or connected with some other book; at times even reminding the editing department of its own rules and the production department of its necessities—such as that an index cannot be made until page proofs exist; in short, imagining and forestalling every disaster.

Part of the permanent muddle in publishing is said to be due to the large turnover in the lower ranks; part is always said to be "unheard of in our firm." But many an experienced author, who in his other business relations finds no cause to complain, will tell you that he is "having publisher trouble," usually of this functional sort suggestive of misrule in the Balkans.

The root of the evil in publishing, as the contributors to the present symposium make plain, lies in its economics. Here is a small business that would like to be at once a profession and an industry. It cannot be the one, lacking the urgent duties and social rewards of a profession; and it can scarcely grow into an industry as long as it lacks control of both supply and outlet.

The young writer who reads that "4,441 is a pretty large number of copies of a novel to sell," and who reflects that this statement is made in a country of 170 million people who claim literacy and are more prosperous than any other, begins to wonder who is the madman—himself for writing novels or his publisher for thinking he owns a *business*.

The writer will in fact find the madness proclaimed in Chester Kerr's well-known report on university presses. These are publishing houses favored by tax exemption and annual subsidy, which should permit them either to balance their books or to reduce the price of those they print. But no: "We publish the smallest editions at the greatest cost, and on these we place the highest prices and then we try to market them to the people who can least afford them. This is madness."

The phrase "marketing of books" is in itself a paradox, a rebuke to sanity. *What* marketing of books? Tradition and a faith in things not seen maintain the bookstore, which the trade calls an outlet; actually, it is a bottleneck, a plugged-up medicine dropper. The census reports some 2,900 bookstores, defined as stores doing more than half of their business in books. Greeting cards, novelties, records, knitting wool fill up the other half, so that publishers count only some 800 to 1,000 as "effective bookstores." The trade consoles itself with the axiom that the United States is "not a reading country." If hamburgers were as inaccessible as books, the United States would have to be put down as "not an eating country."

From this defeatism it appears that publishing is not only sick and mad, but blind. For Americans read voraciously and incessantly. Beginning with advertising and going on to newspapers, comics, magazines, and free literature, the American citizen is more nearly saturated with print than the citizen of any other nation. What book publishers have not recognized, or have not been willing to deal with, is the need to make natural curiosity and common reading habits lead to book buying. Books must compete with the abundance of cheap fare, with the intellectual free lunch: the American newspaper brings, in addition to news, a virtual weekend book; the mail brings a mass of matter, eye-catching, informative, usually well-written; while every group activity, from school to stockholding, in which man, woman, or child engages supplies him with a newsletter, bulletin, or report, which the obedient creature treasures and reads.

This is the daily flood which the would-be book industry professes to divert by sending out a few dozen men into a few hundred narrow passageways called bookstores, to persuade the hard-pressed owner to risk taking "two of Prokosch, ten of Waugh." The bookseller is caught between the rent of his poky shop, the high cost of shipping and accounting, and the vagueness of the public mind—the mind which would forget the name Lucky Strike in a week if unprompted by ads. In this literal and figurative box, a bookseller would be a fool to stock anything but bestsellers and college dictionaries. Which means that the trade's effort at marketing concentrates on persuading him that some new work will be a bestseller. This is done by posters, stickers, and gimmicks (see Mr. Boardman's excellent essay on promotion), as well as by declarations that X dollars is being spent on So-and-So's book—hence, it must sell. This goes on while at the home office So-and-So is being told that advertising never sells a book and that he will be lucky if 4,441 copies of his work are disposed of—lucky because if the firm recovers its cash outlay (not the overhead) it can afford to publish So-and-So's next work.

Meanwhile, the bookseller has been sitting up late to mail out leaflets prepared by the publisher and imprinted with the retailer's address. Everybody then waits. Customers come in, some of them ask for outlandish titles—i.e., not in stock—which they have seen reviewed. The shop man, not always a bookish person, is puzzled but sends off an order. This is the fatal stroke which slays all parties: the publisher is ruined by the demand for single copies, the bookseller is burdened now and forced later to return unsold copies to the publisher, and the

customer is persuaded once again that going into a bookstore is an experience for the damned. "Where in hell,"
asked Al Smith, "would I go and buy a book?" The act
is, in effect, un-American. With luck, the balked reader
will get his book in two weeks; in five, if it was published
by the Blotto University Press.

Out of this asinine comedy grew the book clubs. They
at least dispose of some 50 million copies of books annu-
ally, and their system encourages a certain regularity in
book consumption. But book clubs are not enough,
which is why publishers keep sentimentalizing over the
vanishing bookseller, knowing all the time that the only
source of publishing profits is subsidiary rights, nowadays mostly book-club adoption.

The system of Dr. Tarr and Professor Fether was divine
common sense in comparison with the mechanics of this
highly conscious and civilized industry. But the most
astonishing thing about it is that, being animated by a
deep faith in the importance of books, these economic
cripples and demented merchandisers manage to bring
out nearly every kind of good book that the country
produces, including poetry. Bestsellers and book clubs
carry the rest.

In the face of this devotion to culture and gambling,
criticism is virtually reduced to silence. A modest author
can only murmur the hope to lead all "the rest"—the rest
and not the remainder. And yet, for the sake of that same
culture a few words must be said aloud.

When publishing really wants to become an industry,
it will do two things—develop a marketing technique
and encourage technological improvement in book production. Except for the autographing party, there has

scarcely been a new idea in printing and publishing since Gutenberg—well, since Mergenthaler. Talk to a publisher about the absurdity, in 1957, of handling galleys, and he looks as shocked as if you doubted the rotundity of the earth. Man can split the atom, but not that unmanageable sheet of paper; machines can be made to clear the bank balances of a whole city, but the typographical errors in our books still have to be put in by hand. Where is the electronic, high-fidelity book harvester? The printers today are to publishing what the railroad men are to rail transportation—the dead hand.[2]

The next phase of the revolution should occur in the design, format, and weight of books. American books are thick, heavy, ill-proportioned, unattractive. The lettering, the color schemes, the "art" on jackets or covers are inexcusably commonplace when not downright ugly: compare with the native product its English edition. A point which is not the joke it used to be is that one can put two or three English books in the shelf space occupied by a single American volume. What is more, the English book can be held in one hand. A modern book should be as light and handy and eye-gladdening as a package of perfume, and far more so than a General Motors car. Our book competitions reward conventional merits and perpetuate a depressing uniformity.

Finally, the industry ought to accept its role as a business, and seek strength instead of being a semiprofession with only a halfhearted longing for power and a taste

2. In 1971 the printing industry *seems* to be on the verge of a typesetting revolution wherein galley proofs, page proofs, and much other familiar impedimenta of seeing a book through the press will be swept away. But the marketing practices against which Mr. Barzun inveighs in this essay are, alas, still just as much in need of reform as when he wrote.—Editor

for demiethics. The change might begin in austerity: cutting out futile gimmicks, omitting compulsive lunching, and giving up coauthorship. A firm that exacted standards of competence and completion in work submitted to it would not have to mobilize three people to put a manuscript into shape, thus committing itself to the habit of pulling out of shape the other, acceptable manuscripts—both operations quite unknown to British, French, German, Italian, Swiss, and Scandinavian publishers.

The manpower thus gained could be used in the invention of continually new forms of publicity and promotion—as is done for other products. The trade proclaims that "every book is different," but no one would know this from the jacket blurbs. The reader is not "sold" because he is rarely addressed and often insulted. Why must every author's harried or flirtatious face appear on his book's backside? Why must "opinion" copies be sent out, with coy letters, to opinionated men (always the same), who either refuse an opinion or give one—always the same? Why, in short, the rigmarole inside the trade instead of outside, where it might compete with nylons and vodka in dazzling the buyer?

For every book that sells, virtually unaided, 5,000 to 10,000 copies, there are surely 25,000 to 30,000 readers. The paperbacks prove not only that small books and low prices bring readers, but also that the form of distribution notifies these readers of a book's existence. Hence, books should be thrown in the way of readers and advertised institutionally, *en masse,* in media remote from the purely literary life, until their omnipresence breaks in on the general daydream of unfulfilled desire. For the cheaper books there should be automatic vending machines everywhere, the need for books in the country depot being as great as for stale sandwiches and metallic orangeade. The suggestion will horrify only those who have failed to notice that a habitual reader, like a habitual smoker or drinker, will take anything rather than not indulge his vice.

(And, speaking of drink, the book industry of the future will have to either make a special campaign among the intelligentsia or make package deals with distillers; for the same intellectuals who deplore the country's lack of literary culture seldom buy a book, although they seldom go without a drink.)

These hints toward a reformation can easily be bettered, transfigured, by someone with imagination and knowledge who will care not about books but about business, someone who will be aesthetically offended by the miseries of publishing. At the moment, any change is clearly impossible, and so is the trade; that is why I think almost any change would work.

[1957]

10 Quote 'em Is Taboo

I do not know whether the readers of the *Saturday Review* have ever seen that great natural sight, an error creeping into a text, but if they have been attentive during the past twenty years they must have seen the comparable feat of a page creeping into a book. I refer to the page marked "Acknowledgments," which is now found in almost all works except fiction and which lists the author's debt to publishers for quotations.

The casual reader may suppose that such a page is a sign of proper feeling. He does not know what agony has been mixed with the substance of that uninviting block of print. He cannot guess its subversive implications; and so I must tell him.

When a book is done—a work of scholarship, it may be, or of polemic or of popularization—the writer heaves a sigh, limbers up his joints, and counts the days of respite—three weeks or a month in normal times—before he must brace himself again for reading proof. But this breathing spell is broken into almost at once by a letter from his publishers asking him to obtain his permissions: permissions, that is, for the words he has borrowed from contemporary authors. Say the book is three hundred pages in length and numbers thirty such quotations. One in every ten pages does not seem an excessive reliance on the work of others. The man who quotes is not a drone, and he has paid his fellows tribute by naming them in the text or in footnotes. But he is apparently a sinner nonetheless, and he must climb his purgatory.

First he must look up the names and addresses of the firms that publish what he has used; then he must copy out again his thirty quotations, and wrap up each in a separate letter addressed to the appropriate permissions editor: ninety cents postage and a good day's work *plus* trouble to come.

But why, you will interrupt, cannot the man's publisher act for him? It isn't done. The story is that if an author asks, he is given the right. If a publisher asked, he might have to pay for it. This is known as *esprit de corps.* Again you will wonder why there aren't printed forms for the purpose. Horrors! No author can hope for a civil answer to a printed form. The author is the human personality incarnate and he must never give a hint that publishing is a mere business. Never!—even though in reply to his personal letter certain publishers will send him a printed sheet the size of a bedspread, filled with questions about the motives behind his wishing to quote.

I do not want to exaggerate: it *is* true that a few publishers say, "Yes, go ahead and quote." Among those few some manage to say, "We're delighted you want to use a passage from our Mr. Blankinsop." But the rest variously throw up hurdles—everything from a kind of "H'm, we'll see after we've talked to the F.B.I." to a bland denial that there is or was such a book as the one cited.

What is even worse is the prim washing of hands: "We did originally publish *Never Again,* but copyright has been transferred to Scandal House, Inc." Our author writes to Scandal House. In a week comes the reply, "When Mr. Doolittle came to us, he elected to keep control over copyright, and permissions is in his own hands. You should address him at Shakedown Cottage, Provincetown, Mass." Out goes another letter re-re-requoting the now hateful passage from *Never Again*. The envelope comes back stamped: Addressee Unknown. Then begins the telephone hunt among literary friends, "Where the devil is Doolittle spending the summer? What's his permanent address?" *Who's Who* doesn't help because he hasn't a permanent address, a precaution equally worthy of praise and cursing. Finally, a last random shot hits the mark—word from *Mrs.* Doolittle: "Of course John is willing to have you quote him. Let us know when the new book is out." This is so kind, so far beyond abandoned hope, that it calls for a reply and the postage bill passes the $2.00 mark.

If the quoted authors are English, the business is not only lengthened in time but complicated by international misunderstanding. G. B. Shaw's secretary replies half-petulantly: "[You fool] you are entitled to 150 words *without* permission." Tell that to *our* marines; they want a letter in their files showing that the American writer did ask anyway. They want a document, were it only the musings, scribbled on the back of a menu, of a man who once ran a quarterly into the ground: "Are you sure we published an article by Cecil Syringe? I have no recollection of it, and if we did I haven't an idea in whom copyright is vested. I rather doubt whether *he* would know. Faithfully yours. . . ."

Time is passing; galley proofs are pouring in; copy for the Acknowledgments page is overdue. But not all the returns are in—and besides, the proper wording of that page remains a puzzle. For certain firms insist on a set formula of their own: "The lines from Rufus Brown's

White Heat are quoted by special arrangement with and permission of Tetanus, Spohr, and Company, New York, London, Toronto, and Melbourne." Men of sense armed with courage will disregard this special notation whose wording jibes with none of the others and makes straight listing impossible. What will happen then?—Nothing.

Nothing. Which brings me at last to the question burning in the reader's mind. "Why this maddening oriental punctilio about a few hundred words in quotation marks?" The official answer is that it is all for the author's good, that it strengthens the owner of copyright matter in his control over its use. "Suppose," a publisher once disarmingly said to me, "that you are an unscrupulous hack. You want to enliven your work by using whole pages from better men. You take an essay by E. B. White, put quotation marks around it, and there you are. What's to stop you, unless there is an agreement among reputable publishers to require permission all around?"

Having just snared the last of my thirty letters, I could only mumble, "I see." But my proper answer should have been, "Suppose I bring you a manuscript full of stolen plums: why should you—or any other publisher—publish it? Protect yourselves at first hand by using your judgment instead of my clerical ability."

That would mean really reading the book. Quotations being for a purpose, the purpose declares itself in the context and in no other way. If I write about the drama, I may quote three pages from Shaw and be no plagiarist. If I quote for ornament, I should be brief. And if I begin, "As Churchill aptly says . . ." following it up with his Collected Speeches, I should be jailed. Makers of anthologies, plainly, must ask and pay for the privilege of reprinting copyrighted work. In any given instance, the law's reasonable man can tell what is going on. If the law avers that it cannot, then "the law is a ass." (By permission of Charles Dickens's heirs and assigns.)

Whatever its origin or dim purpose, this new legalism is not entirely a joke, and I am not protesting merely against the nuisance and waste of time. I am even willing to overlook the sense of might with right which a permissions department must give to unhappy publishers in their tribal war against authors. But from the point of view of general culture I see some serious consequences and, chiefly, a hindrance to the circulation of ideas in their best form. If each living quotation entails so much work, the intending user will ask himself, Is it worth it? and cut down his thirty to ten.

But that is not all. The establishing of acknowledgments in our books is but another sign of our modern smoothiness based on false feelings and false human relations. The false feeling is the inflation of gratefulness on a trivial pretext; the false relation is the setting up of the middleman above the thing in which he meddles. Not that I reprove gratitude nor urge a return to literary piracy. On the contrary, I feel very strongly that cultural debts come first among debts of honor. But as a writer my thanks properly go to other writers and not to "owners of copyright." When I name the maker of a fine phrase, I am not "paying him for his trouble"; I am only voicing my pleasure and loyally indicating its source. If that is so, I see no reason to advertise his publisher into the bargain. True, the publisher indirectly helped me to come across the phrase, but then he took his reward in cash. And if I am bound to thank him besides, where does the obligation stop? The printer, the proofreader, the office boy—all were indispensable, too.

That this modern sentimentality is not the simple

result of the legal mind at work can be seen in the effusions of love which nowadays adorn every kind of printed thing. Reproductions of great art, for instance, do not come to us from the pencil of Leonardo, but "owing to the great kindness and unfailing courtesy of Miss Belladonna Jones, Curator of the Something-or-Other Museum." Is it because she is normally rude that we fall on our knees when her courtesy holds out? Or does she own the paintings more possessively than do the trustees of the museum or the city fathers?

To be sure, librarians, curators, and publishers can sometimes become the author's real colleagues and friends. I have been so lucky in this regard that I can speak quite impersonally of that other, artificial lather of gratitude. It is precisely to distinguish the two that words should be used with care. Otherwise the currency of thanks will become worthless, like the old-time dedications to lords and princes. And the result is not hard to foresee: first we misdirect public attention and then we debase the instinct of appreciation. There is already a pretty general temptation to consider the conductor more important than the composer, the cellophane more desirable than the goods, the sun tan more appealing than the face. When this cosmetic attitude affects art, it is time to overhaul our verbal habits. There is, after all, nothing hidden or difficult about a right judgment in the matter. What we want to know under a picture is who made it and where it may be seen. In books we want to know who said that true thing so brightly and in what work. Scholarship may require a more exact assignment of time and place, but even scholarship can be cluttered up with needless kissing of hands to literary executors and keepers of air-conditioned manuscripts.

A hint from the past can help to keep us straight: we should never have had Burton's *Anatomy of Melancholy* if he had had to ask for permissions; and Lamb, who thoughtfully pillaged him, would probably be blacklisted by our best publishers. Obviously Montaigne, who said: "I have gathered a nosegay of other men's flowers and only the thread that binds them is my own" was just that "unscrupulous hack" imagined by my legal friend. As for Sir Thomas Browne and the author of *Moby Dick,* they would still be unpublished: the answers to their letters would not yet be in.

[1945]

NOTE: In the twenty-five years that have passed since Jacques Barzun wrote this essay, first-class postal rates have more than doubled, but in partial compensation the paranoia of publishers with regard to permissions has also eased slightly. At their annual meeting next following original publication of the essay, the Association of American University Presses decided to allay some of the permissions anxiety of other publishers by declaring publicly that scholars need not ask permission to quote from works published by its member presses so long as whole units (like poems, charts, or chapters) were not taken and so long as the quotation was employed for the usual scholarly purposes of criticism, review, evaluation, or citation of authority. This of course was well within what the law permitted, but its reiteration by the AAUP has had a salutary effect on permissions work. The 1947 Reciprocal Agreement on Permissions has been revised from time to time (it originally specified a maximum of one thousand words for "fair" quotation, and this misguided limitation has been dropped), but the agreement is still in effect, having been signed by most of the sixty-odd presses belonging to the AAUP.—EDITOR

11   The Screening Mimis

5 January 1960

DEAR MR. AIGHED:

As you may know, the FOB network has steadily endeavored to increase its public service function by offering in nonsponsored time programs of lasting educational value. On one of these programs, "Sit and Think," it has been customary to have notable authors read an article of theirs on some issue currently under discussion.

We have just come across your provocative essay in *Foreign Affairs* entitled "Disciplines for Diplomats," and we should like to feature it as soon as practicable on "Sit and Think." Since the program occupies a 15-minute spot, from 7:15 to 7:30 on Sunday morning, the reading time available is 13½ minutes, and this in turn means that your article will have to be somewhat shortened. You may want to do this yourself, or we will gladly have one of our experienced editors here in the office suggest the necessary cuts for your approval. The tape can be made at your home or in our studio, at your convenience.

Hoping for the pleasure of hearing from you soon and favorably,

Sincerely yours,
DOUGLAS DOISTER
Director of Public Service Programs

11 January 1960

DEAR MR. DOISTER:

I am touched by your kind interest in my recent article on the training of diplomats and I wish I could accept your invitation to read it over the air.

But I must point out that it runs to 4,500 words, which would take about 35 minutes to read. When therefore you speak of "cutting" it to fit into 13½ minutes, you really mean discarding nearly two-thirds of the substance. Having just reread the piece, I cannot persuade myself that it is too long for what I have to say, though I could with some effort omit, say, 500–600 words and thus shorten the reading time by four or five minutes.

Any reduction such as you require would call for a complete rewriting from scratch.

Yours faithfully,
ARNOLD AIGHED

*
* *

15 January 1960

DEAR MR. AIGHED:

I would not presume to argue with you over the contents of your essay. You no doubt know best how long it should be. But I am sorry that you adopt an uncooperative line about editing which is all too common among writers, and which shows that you do not appreciate the exigencies of the new and powerful medium which is TV.

Surely you want your ideas to reach millions of people rather than the few thousand who read the specialized magazine for which you wrote your article. If I add that we will make an exception in your case and print for free distribution your article *in full,* will you not reconsider and allow us to extract the 13½ essential minutes?

Hoping for the pleasure of your prompt and favorable reply,

Yours sincerely,
DOUGLAS DOISTER
Director of Public Service Programs

*
*   *

27 January 1960

DEAR MR. DOISTER:

I am sorry to persist in my refusal and even more sorry that I did not succeed in conveying to you the grounds of it.

In declining to be excerpted as you wish, I am not "adopting a line." The reason for my response, which I am not surprised to hear is common in writers, is simply that I understand the exigencies of an old and powerful medium known as expository prose. These exigencies you apparently fail to appreciate. Instead you think it is a public service to present an incomplete or disjointed argument, expecting the listener (I suppose) to sit and think it out.

You say that I surely want to reach millions of people. That depends on whether the emphasis is put on "reach" much more than on "millions." I will not, by the way, try to guess how many millions are likely to be awake at 7:15 on Sunday morning. Let me only remark that to all appearances your good deed is being done by stealth, as enjoined by the Scriptures.

Please understand that I am not telling you indirectly what you should do: I am only trying to show you the gap between your large professions and your meager performance.

Yours sincerely,
ARNOLD AIGHED

*
* *

10 February 1960

DEAR MR. AIGHED:

When George Baker introduced us the other day he said something about your high sales resistance to TV and told me not to bring up the subject, least of all socially. Well, you remember, I didn't. But right now I'm sure I've got a proposition that will make you feel quite different about the whole subject.

You've probably never heard of "Talkfest." It's new. But I'm sure that when I explain it you'll fall for it. At long last it's the program we've all been waiting for, where people who can talk and people who like to hear *and see* good talk can get together by means of the new and powerful medium which is TV.

"Talkfest" gives you all the freedom of a real conversation. It starts at 2:00 P.M. on Saturday and goes on, free and uninhibited, till Sunday midnight. The people on the show any weekend wander in freely any time they want, and wander out again when they like—just as the listeners do, or for that matter the denizens of an old-world *salon*.

Same with the subject—anything goes. I'm on the show merely to put in the plugs for my sponsors every half hour and to ask a question or two when things look like they're beginning to flag. I do not m.c. or moderate. My job comes ahead of time, in providing the right mix, I mean inviting the people who'll catalyze each other—and then you're off!

Now think it over and give me a ring to say which weekend you'll go on. George told me how busy you are with your new book, on foreign policy, is it? Well, I promise you "Talkfest" is an experience that won't set you back. It will give you a lift. And when the time comes it'll do your book a lot of good. So spare us even just a Sunday. We'd want you to come about noon sharp so as to be able to wander in about 1:30, after a little briefing by my assistant, Miss Chorio. That way there's no strain.

I'm asking you first so I can line up the others. The balance I have in mind for you would be perfect: as a heavy, thoughtful type and not likely to go off the handle, you need someone vivacious, unpredictable—a woman, preferably an actress type or even an actress. We might ask Diana Cecily. And then, just for kicks and to keep the audience guessing, someone with a bit of mystery and a man-about-town flavor. There is a Prince Detropoff you probably know, who claims he is a grandnephew of the tsar. He has great personality.

You see the pains I'm taking over you and your prejudice against TV. Say you'll come; all you have to do is tell me when.

As ever yours,
RALPH ROISTER

P.S. Of course, it's none of my business, but let me just add that it would be great if when I get you three together you could spend a good bit of your time discussing the future of the arts in America.

*
* *

19 February 1960

DEAR MR. AIGHED:

Excuse my delay in answering your letter of last month about what you called the exigencies of writers, which you think I do not appreciate.

I am sure I appreciate them as fully as you do. I was a writer once myself, and an editor after that, and my experience suggests that every writer who is worth his salt takes a very humble view of his work and knows he can be improved by competent editing.

In fact—and I say it to you without offense—I think that adapting to the format of a TV show, long or short, is for any writer a wonderful discipline. I know it is not usual in your line of work, where there is plenty of time to read and plenty of paper and print to expend on scholarly subjects. But we live in a dynamic world, and in TV especially, where broadcast time is expensive, it's bound to be short. That is why it must be used with the utmost efficiency, no matter what older habits may permit elsewhere.

Accordingly, I am sorry we cannot see eye to eye about your article which we liked so much in this office, but I send you good wishes all the same. Should you ever change your mind about "Sit and Think," please let me know.

> Yours sincerely,
> DOUGLAS DOISTER
> Director of Public Service Programs

*

* *

29 February 1960

DEAR MR. ROISTER:

You are kind to invite me to appear on "Talkfest" in such distinguished company.

It is true that I like conversation and would do almost anything to obtain it, but I am afraid that the absence of limits which is the main feature of "Talkfest" would unnerve me to the point where I might wander out freely whenever my fellow participants began to open their mouths, returning only when I had something to say. Even if this should prove acceptable to you as an attractive novelty, I could not undertake to keep it up faithfully from about noon sharp to midnight more or less.

The truth is that in any public performance in which I am to take part I want a moderator, with a gavel and a watch, to open and close the proceedings. Besides, I am occasionally vivacious too, and I may need to be called to order. It is only when required to talk about the future of the arts in America that my spirits droop, and then I need a moderator to cut me off before the audience notices it. For these few public services I would willingly give up all the half-hour interruptions of sponsor-worship.

My best to George when you see him.

Yours faithfully,
ARNOLD AIGHED

*
* *

29 February 1960

DEAR MR. DOISTER:

One final word in reply to your last, in which you chose to turn our difference of opinion into an argument against writers and scholars as represented by my unworthy self.

In so doing you abandoned your case, for I remind you that it was you who sought me out, not I who submitted my work to you. I have never objected to editing; I did and do object to abridgment by two-thirds. You are the one who claimed to perform a public service; I merely pointed out, when challenged, that garbling ideas is not a service. You put the word "Think" into a program so scheduled that it might better be called "Came the Dawn." I contented myself with showing that you do not understand the proper conditions either of thought or of its reception by the general public.

There is one further point I have not yet touched on. If Gibbon had just published the first volume of *The Decline and Fall,* you would doubtless ask him to whittle it down to the essential 13½ minutes. To which he would reply: "I can indeed furnish a text on my subject which will occupy these few moments, but that entails a fresh piece of work for which I must be paid."

This would not be naïveté on Gibbon's part, for how could he know that the public service which sheds luster on the great network must rest on a broad base of unpaid talent? It would be necessary to explain to him that broadcasting time is expensive enough as it is without adding a charge that might well stop the world from being dynamic. Fortunately for public service, writers are so besotted that the millions they sometimes dream of are readers, not dollars. Hence the custom which makes it low and shameful to cadge a consultation from a doctor or lawyer, but normal and proper to ask a writer or lecturer to do something for the sole delight of being asked.

These are but a few points to sit and think about.

Yours faithfully,
ARNOLD AIGHED

*

*   *

2 April 1960

DEAR MR. AIGHED:

We have been looking at the copy of your new book, which has just come from your publishers. We think it is a wonderful book, the kind our listeners I am sure would enjoy hearing thoroughly discussed.

That's why I am asking you to give us the pleasure of attending the session of "Take the Rap," which will be devoted to your work, one week from next Thursday at 11:00 P.M. in our studios. I hope to greet you there myself.

As you know the "critics" on this program, now in its sixth year, are not all professionals. The layman, who is so important in a democracy, is represented also, usually by one businessman, one housewife, and one teen-ager. This will be particularly appropriate for your book, since foreign policy is something which closely concerns all these occupations and age groups.

Our regular critic and moderator, John DeTester, will unfortunately be on a lecture tour, but we have a promise from Mr. Kurt Erfloh, the dance critic of *Terpsichore*, that he will be delighted to stand in for John.

We look forward to your call accepting the date, as well as to meeting you and having you autograph our office copy of your marvelous book.

Cordially,
(MRS.) SUSAN ROISTER-DOISTER

5 April 1960

DEAR MRS. ROI ....

[1960]

Envoy:
Of Making Books

"I have seen books made," says Montaigne, "of things neither studied nor understood; the author entrusting the research to learned friends . . . himself content to supply industry in tying together these faggots of unknown origin: at least the paper and ink are his." We have not quite reached this degree of delegation in composing our modern books, but the ironic complaint still has point. It is so easy to make what looks like a book, by taking notes instead of thought and by following an outline instead of an inspiration.

Everything—time, current practice, and even our scholarly virtues—tempts us to the imposture; for is not scholarship based on the extant literature, and are we not bound to submit our work for criticism, in parts, to all our learned friends? The result is a marvelous anonymity of tone, equaled only by a noble avoidance of risk. We please by not displeasing, and we achieve through collective effort the professional glaze of that famous periodical whose articles, it was said, had to be approved by ten men.

That was not the way of Montaigne. We should more frequently remind ourselves that he wrote his essays first and added the quotations afterwards—most of them, indeed, posthumously. And again, that like so many others still readable, he sought chiefly to please himself, setting down his thought eccentrically, without an outline or a file of cards, despite his love of order; and yet managed, somehow, to fashion a piece of time-resisting work.

He is a particularly good example in these days, because we cannot explain him and excuse ourselves by reference to the quiet leisurely times in which he lived. We know that he had to do his thinking between freebooting raids on his house, and that he observed life while it hung on the whim of pestilence or the good will of armed fanatics. In spite of this, and though "surrounded by thousands of books," he used his precedents as starting points, not as havens of certitude. We who are not yet so enveloped by strife, have contracted timidity from another cause: we want to be right. We dread the reader who will pounce upon an error of fact, an unfamiliar thought, a naïve sentiment. To purchase his thin feasting smiles we give up our only chances of being largely true—by long turning over of simple experience, by pondering what we read, by informed divination.

The upshot is that we too are surrounded by thousands of books—learned, semilearned, popular; and hardly anywhere in this mass can we find Emerson's scholar, man thinking. In all these works, short or long, the effort has gone into manufacturing: the publisher, his readers, the editorial hands, the librarians, the colleagues, the wife, and the author have *conspired* to put together a book; checked and double-checked the matter; made an industrial product of "faggots of unknown origin." But the living speech of a true witness is absent.

[1946]

Acknowledgments

Permission to reprint a number of the essays in this volves is gratefully acknowledged. The following list gives the original facts of publication for all essays here republished.

"Advice to a Young Writer" was a private letter to a high school student, published in the 1969 issue of *Flight,* a periodical of Saint Edward High School, Cleveland.

"A Writer's Discipline" appeared originally as "Calamophobia, or Hints toward a Writer's Discipline" in *The Writer's Book,* edited by Helen Hull and sponsored by the Authors Guild (New York: Harper and Bros., 1950).

"English As She's Not Taught" was published in the December 1953 issue of the *Atlantic Monthly.*

"A Few Words on a Few Words" was published in the Summer 1974 issue of the *Columbia Forum.*

"Food for the *NRF*" appeared as "Food for the N.R.F., or 'My God! What Will You Have?'" in the *Partisan Review,* November/December 1953.

"Lincoln the Writer" was published in the *Saturday Evening Post* on 14 February 1959 under the title "Lincoln the Literary Genius."

"Poe As Proofreader" appeared as "A Note on the Inadequacy of Poe As a Proofreader and of His Editors As French Scholars" in the *Romanic Review,* February 1970.

"The Bibliographer and His Absence of Mind" appeared as "The Book, the Bibliographer, and the Absence of Mind" in the Winter 1969 issue of the *American Scholar*.

"Behind the Blue Pencil" appeared as "Behind the Blue Pencil: Censorship or Creeping Creativity?" in the Summer 1985 issue of the *American Scholar*.

"Paradoxes of Publishing," originally entitled "The Anatomy of Book Publishing," was published in the *New Leader* on 13 May 1957.

"Quote 'em Is Taboo" was published in the *Saturday Review of Literature* for 22 September 1945.

"The Screening Mimis," originally entitled "TV in the World of Letters," appeared in the Spring 1960 issue of the *American Scholar*.

Finally, "Of Making Books" was originally published in the summer 1946 issue of the same journal.